BIRMINGHAM: SHAPING THE CITY

RIBA #H# **Publishing**

Birmingham City Council

© RIBA ENTERPRISES LTD AND BIRMINGHAM CITY COUNCIL, 2008

Published by RIBA Publishing, part of RIBA Enterprises Ltd
15 Bonhill Street
London EC2P 2EA

ISBN 978 1 85946 245 4
Stock Code 60397

British Library Cataloguing in Publications Data
A catalogue record for this book is available from the British Library.

Author: Ben Flatman
Photo Editor: Craig Holmes
Craig's archive can be found at www.imagesofbirmingham.co.uk
Publisher: Steven Cross
Project Editor: Susan George
Editor: Ian McDonald
Designed by Kneath Associates
Printed and bound by Cambridge University Press

Photographs and illustrations have been supplied by imagesofbirmingham. co.uk. Additional picture research was under-taken by Craig Holmes with the exception of some of the case study images in Chapter 3 which have been supplied separately and are credited accordingly within the text.

Every effort has been made to contact copyright holders. Queries should be addressed to RIBA Publishing, 15 Bonhill Street, London EC2P 2EA

RIBA Publishing is part of RIBA Enterprises Ltd.
www.ribaenterprises.com

Front cover © Craig Holmes
Photographer: Craig Holmes/Images of Birmingham.co.uk

CONTENTS

BIRMINGHAM: SHAPING THE CITY

MORLEY VON STERNBERG

FOREWORD

SUNAND PRASAD

Royal Institute of British Architects, President 2007 – 2009

Birmingham is a city with a long history of radical and ambitious regeneration. From the brash confidence of its Victorian heyday, to the optimism of the1960s, Birmingham has enthusiastically embraced the big challenges and opportunities. Over the past two decades Birmingham has undergone a transformation that after a period of decline recaptures the best of the spirit of its past. This change has been underpinned by the quality of the city's new architecture and urban design, the best of which is presented in this book.

The turning point in Birmingham's recent history can be traced back to the Highbury Initiative of 1988, which brought together architects, planners and experts from many other disciplines. Coming from both within the UK and further afield, those in attendance included rising stars such as Terry Farrell and Will Alsop, who would go on to become leading exponents of new and contrasting approaches to urban design. The recommendations that grew from this symposium provided the basis for one of the most concerted and carefully considered recent programmes of urban regeneration in the UK.

During the late 1980s and early 1990s, Birmingham was a living demonstration to the rest of the UK's struggling regional cities of how to take their destinies into their own hands, and that managing decline was not their only option. With schemes such as the International Convention Centre and Centenary Square, Birmingham pioneered an entrepreneurial approach to urban regeneration that combined new city-centre based service industries with revitalised public spaces and new architecture. Through the 'Percent for Art' scheme, sculpture and other forms of public art were placed at the heart of the regeneration agenda.

The transformation is evident for all who visit Birmingham today. The city is unrecognisable from twenty years ago. The hostile, car-dominated, anti-human roads and roundabouts have been transformed. The new squares, the canalside and other public places are alive with people and activity. There remain considerable challenges and great opportunities and with a new city-centre masterplan under development by Urban Initiatives, there is the chance to build the foundations for another two decades of change. As one of the UK's youngest and most diverse cities, it is possible that Birmingham will again be setting an agenda that others will follow. Great architecture and urban design must – and surely will – be at the heart of the life of this evolving future city.

PREFACE

MIKE WHITBY
Leader of Birmingham City Council

Birmingham is a global city with a local heart which is held in increasingly high regard on the world stage. Our economy is ranked number 71 among global cities, and we continue to forge economic, political, cultural and technological links with the powerhouses of the future.

Urban regeneration is one area where Birmingham serves as a beacon to cities everywhere. We continue to turn our city centre into an international showcase, with some of the UK's most innovative and iconic architecture, beautifully illustrated in this book.

At the European Property Awards in 2005, Birmingham was named European City of the Future, recognising the fact that we are always ready to embrace and encourage further progress.

Our new City Centre Masterplan is now being drawn up, along with tailored prospectuses for the next phase of regeneration in the rest of Birmingham.

And we are welcoming £17 billion of regeneration in the next 10 years, including exciting projects such as The Cube and the V-Building.

All of these developments will add a new dimension to Birmingham's skyline and improve the built environment in which we live, work and socialise.

We celebrate our achievements to date, and invite new contributions to help build our future. Birmingham fosters creative thinking around architecture, and provides a broad canvas for innovative ideas to become reality.

I hope you will enjoy what you find here.

< Yeoville Thomason's Council
House, Victoria Square
PAUL WARD/ IMAGES OF BIRMINGHAM

∨ Fort Dunlop, redeveloped by
Urban Splash and ShedKM
Architects in 2007
WWW.ADRIAN-BURROWS.CO.UK

ACKNOWLEDGEMENTS

I would like to thank Steven, Sue and Anna at RIBA Publishing and Craig Holmes for their help over the course of writing the book as well as Philip Singleton at Birmingham City Council for his support over several years. Many thanks also to the countless people who have contributed images and data for the project profiles in Chapter 3 and offered me their time through interviews and advice elsewhere in the book.

I would like to express particular thanks to my parents in Birmingham, and Jot, Glen and Louis in London for their unfailing love and support. Also many thanks to my beloved grandmother Vera for her motivational encouragement and impatience to see this book published! And finally, thanks to my Bhavna for her wise words, help and faith throughout.

Ben Flatman

< The Birmingham Wheel is
reflected in the facade of the
Hyatt Regency Hotel
CRAIG HOLMES/IMAGES OF BIRMINGHAM

PUBLISHING PARTNERS

We would like to thank all of the companies listed here who have generously supported the publication of this wonderful book.

The development and regeneration of Birmingham is a success story for all those involved – from those working within the City Council, the investors, developers, architects and contractors who have supported and backed the redevelopment plans, to, ultimately, the local businesses, people and communities.

None of what you will see and read in this book could have been achieved without the support and encouragement of companies like those listed here. We thank them for their support and look forward to working with them in the future.

Sunand Prasad and
Councillor Mike Whitby

< Benoy's Bullring Shopping
Centre, opened 2003
CRAIG HOLMES/IMAGES OF BIRMINGHAM

ADVANTAGE WEST MIDLANDS	ARGENT	THE BALLYMORE GROUP

Advantage West Midlands is the Regional Development Agency (RDA) for the West Midlands and one of nine RDAs in England. Our role is to lead the economic development of the West Midlands Region, working alongside public, private and voluntary sector partners to help our region to prosper. We build upon our region's many strengths and address our unique challenges. Our key task is to lead the development and delivery of the West Midlands Economic Strategy (WMES), the framework for our region's growth. Through working in partnership, we speak with one voice for the region and make a far greater impact than we would acting in isolation.

We have an annual budget of over £300 million to invest in the West Midlands Region and, at any one time, we manage around 2,500 projects which change the lives of people across our region. We drive economic development by identifying where we can make the greatest impact, either by targeting specific needs or investing in success.

Argent has become a leading practitioner of city centre regeneration with a strong track record in complex, city centre, mixed use regeneration schemes that combine offices, shops, hotels, cafes, restaurants and residential.

Argent focuses on just a few, exceptional schemes at any one time and supports these major projects with speculative development and world class public realm.

In addition to Brindleyplace, Argent has been involved in the rejuvenation of Piccadilly in Manchester; major commercial developments in the City of London and in the Thames Valley and is leading an eight million sq ft regeneration scheme at King's Cross in London.

The first buildings at King Cross will be ready for occupation in 2010. By then, Argent will part own, manage or be developing a portfolio of over 10 million square feet, with an end value of over £3.5 billion.

Ballymore is one of Europe's largest property development and investment companies. It is privately-owned with principle offices in Dublin and London. It currently has over 4.5m sq m in development across Europe – the UK, Ireland, The Czech Republic, Germany and Slovakia.

Ballymore celebrates its 25th Anniversary this year. Founded by Sean Mulryan, Ballymore has an International reputation for quality, not just in terms of buildings but quality in all aspects of developing new communities. Ballymore strives to enhance the local environment and enrich the local community wherever it invests.

Commitment to economic sustainability and social responsibility is central to Ballymore's business philosophy.

Ballymore has over 4.5 million sq m of projects under construction or at various stages of the planning process.

As a privately owned business, Ballymore is able to react quickly to opportunities and respond accordingly. It is envisaged that the next 25 years will be as exciting for Ballymore as the first 25 have been.

BEETHAM ORGANIZATION

Beetham Organization is an innovative and dynamic property development company committed to achieving the highest quality of design in all its projects. The opportunity to develop an iconic mixed-use residential hotel tower in the centre of Birmingham was most enthusiastically embraced. The Beetham Tower in Birmingham has become a symbol of Birmingham's successful regeneration, as well as being a catalyst for the City's continued renaissance. Birmingham is an International City and it is entirely fitting that its new buildings should be recognized Internationally. All of the team who have worked on this scheme are proud to have been part of changing the City's skyline and making a positive contribution to the built environment of the City.

THE BIRMINGHAM ALLIANCE

The Birmingham Alliance is a partnership between Hammerson plc, Land Securities Group PLC, and Henderson Global Investors Ltd, formed in February 1999 to carry out the phased redevelopment of 40 acres – equating to some 190,000 m^2 of retail space – in central Birmingham.

The Birmingham Alliance has injected over £600 million into the local economy to date, of which Bullring represents £500 million. Opened in September 2003, Bullring is considered one of the most outstanding examples of sustainable retail-led city centre regeneration in Europe, recognised with over 50 industry awards worldwide.

BIRMINGHAM DEVELOPMENT CO LTD

Birmingham Development Company is the team behind The Mailbox and The Cube in Birmingham city centre.

The company aims to create exclusive developments of an iconic nature which will drive values and attract international attention to Birmingham.

The Mailbox launched in 2000 and brought the first designer stores to the city centre as well as waterside restaurants and café bars; state of the art offices including the BBC TV and Radio studios; 200 luxury rooftop and canalside apartments and two hotels.

The Cube designed by Make architects is intended to be an iconic full stop to The Mailbox with an unforgettable design, prominent public art and an equally exclusive offering, including the city's first rooftop restaurant already let to D&D London, formerly Conran.

CROSBY LEND LEASE

Edgbaston-based developer Crosby Lend Lease has had an exceptional 11 years in the regional property industry, during which time it has delivered £400 million of design-led new homes in Birmingham city centre.

Crosby was the first developer to spot the emerging trend towards city living in Birmingham and set the standard with its pioneering Symphony Court scheme in 1995, which remains one of the city's most prestigious addresses. More recently at The Orion Building – a joint collaboration with international fashion designer John Rocha and BBLB – Crosby's £1.65 million penthouse has redefined apartment living.

Now with more than 12 apartment schemes completed or in progress in Birmingham and beyond, Crosby Lend Lease has consolidated its position as a leading sustainable developer.

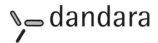

DANDARA

Established in 1988, the Dandara Group is a specialist developer of quality designed, high specification, mixed-use property. Dandara is developing exciting new urban quarters in some of the UK's fastest growing Cities including Birmingham, London, Glasgow, Leeds, Manchester, as well as the Isle of Man and Channel Islands.

Dandara has a passion for delivering great places for everyday life and its projects often demand the integration of commercial, retail and leisure uses. Employing its own work force to ensure the highest levels of build quality and finish, Dandara has steadily and successfully diversified into other markets, providing much sought-after property investment opportunities and assistance with finance, residential letting and furnishing through to full property management.

HOARE LEA

Hoare Lea is an independent, award winning, firm of consulting engineers specialising in mechanical, electrical and environmental engineering. Founded in Birmingham, in 1862, Hoare Lea now employs 700 staff in the UK.

Hoare Lea has specialist design groups to support every aspect of the building environmental brief and can offer expert advice in many specialist areas including acoustics, fire engineering and sustainability.

In Birmingham Hoare Lea has worked, or is currently working, on projects such as Baskerville House, Birmingham Town Hall, Birmingham Library, Brindleyplace, City Park Gate, Colmore Square, The Cube, Orion, Snowhill, Southside, The V Building and many other prominent schemes in and around the City Centre.

ISIS
waterside
regeneration

ISIS

Isis Waterside Regeneration was formed
in 2002 by British Waterways with Igloo
(the regeneration fund of Morley Fund
Management) and AMEC Developments
(now MUSE Developments). Named after
the Egyptian goddess of rejuvenation, Isis
was created to deliver the Government's
vision of an urban renaissance, building
on the natural strength of our waterways
to create mixed, balanced and diverse
genuinely sustainable communities.

Isis work to a business model that
prioritizes people, climate change and
creating great places as the fundamental
drivers of creating added commercial value
to their projects. Fifty per cent of Isis profits
are reinvested in Britain's waterways.

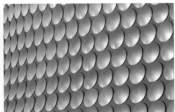

TIMELINE

1156	Peter de Bermingham obtains a market charter from Henry II.
1250	William de Bermingham obtains permission to hold a four-day fair at Whitsun.
1263	First mention of a church on the current site of St Martin's.
1406	First recorded reference to a goldsmith within Birmingham.
1538	Population recorded as being around 1,500 people living in 200 houses.
1642–6	Birmingham supplies the Parliamentarians with arms during the Civil War, emerging with a strong reputation as a metalworking centre.
1650	Birmingham's population is recorded as being 5,372.
1725	Thomas Archer's St Phillip's Church is completed.
1731	Population reaches 23,000.
1760	Population reaches 35,000.
1834	Hansom and Welch's Town Hall opens, becoming one of the first major civic buildings in Birmingham.
1835	Charles Edge's market hall opens in the Bull Ring.
1837	Queen Victoria comes to the throne.
1838	Municipal charter establishes an elected council, adopts 'Forward' as motto. London to Birmingham Railway opens, terminus at Curzon Street.
1839	Police force established.
1841	Pugin's St Chad's Cathedral is completed.
1843	Birmingham School of Art formed as a Government School of Design.
1846	Adderley Park in Saltley opens (4.5 hectares): Birmingham's first public park.
1851	The Improvement Act incorporates powers of old local bodies in the town council, giving it complete control over roads, sewers, lighting and sanitary arrangements, public buildings, markets and baths. Kent Street Baths and Washhouse opens.
1857	Calthorpe Park opens (12.5 hectares).
1861	First public library opens, in Constitution Hill.
1864	Aston Hall and Park opens to the public (20 hectares).
1867	Art gallery opens.
1870	School board started.
1872	First Medical Officer of Health, Dr Hill, appointed.

1872–3	First horse-bus service introduced from Snow Hill to Dudley Port. The first tram lines built by the borough council then leased to the Birmingham Tramway Company.
1873	Joseph Chamberlain becomes mayor. Cannon Hill Park opens (33 hectares).
1874	Aston Villa Football Club founded. First municipal hospital (for fever only).
1875	J. A. Chatwin's remodelled St Martin's in the Bull Ring is completed. The Artisans Dwellings Act allows corporations to acquire, demolish and redevelop slum areas. Clearance begins for the building of Corporation Street. Corporation takes over the supply of gas. Birmingham City Football Club founded. Birmingham Fire Brigade started.
1876	Joseph Chamberlain elected as one of Birmingham's MPs. By-law passed which effectively forbids the building of back-to-back houses. Town takes over the private water supply.
1877	Edward R. Taylor appointed head of the School of Art. An early Arts and Crafts man, he changed teaching methods to emphasise craft skills – with 'Art Laboratories' for subjects such as metalwork.
1878	Private Act of Parliament allows the corporation to take over certain burial grounds in the central ward and make them into public gardens – St Martin's, St Mary's, St George's and St Philip's.
1879	George and Richard Cadbury build new factory at Bournville, 6.5 km from the town. Yeoville Thomason's Council House is formally opened.
1883	John Henry Chamberlain dies suddenly soon after completing the drawings for his finest building, the School of Art.
1885	Birmingham School of Art becomes the first Municipal School of Art. The increased freedom that municipalisation entailed enabled the School to challenge centralised policies of teaching style, methods and content, and to erect in part an alternative Arts and Crafts system working with physical materials.
1889	Birmingham becomes a city. Corporation Street completed.
1890	The School of Jewellery opens in the Jewellery Quarter.
1891	Balsall Heath, Saltley and Harborne incorporated into Birmingham. City takes over the supply of electricity. Aston Webb's Victoria Law Courts open on Corporation Street.

∨ The Birmingham skyline
PAUL WARD/IMAGES OF BIRMINGHAM

∨ The International Convention Centre
BIRMINGHAM LIBRARIES & ARCHIVES

∨ Symphony Hall
NICOLE FROST

1900 The University of Birmingham receives its charter.

1909 Aston Webb's new university campus opens on land donated by Lord Calthorpe.

1901 February, Queen Victoria dies. J. Cuming Walters publishes a series of articles in the Birmingham Daily Gazette entitled 'Scenes in Slumland'; in June, in the face of public pressure, The Housing Committee is formed.

1905 St. Phillip's becomes the city's cathedral.

1918 Architect William Haywood publishes *The Development of Birmingham*, which contains proposals for a new civic centre on Broad Street, an extended central library on Victoria Square and a remodelling of New Street Station.

1938 The Queen Elizabeth Hospital opens in Edgbaston.

1939 Robert Atkinson's Barber Institute is completed. Birmingham International Airport opens at Elmdon; it is owned and run by BCC.

1963 The Ikon begins as a 'gallery without walls' focusing on touring exhibitions.

1964 The new Bull Ring Shopping Centre is opened by the Duke of Edinburgh.

1965 Ikon moves into a glass kiosk in the Bull Ring.

1971 The new Birmingham Rep opens. The Inner Ring Road is completed.

1974 Martin and Chamberlain's Central Library is demolished despite fierce opposition, while John Madin's replacement nearby is opened by Harold Wilson.

1976 The National Exhibition Centre opens.

1984 The new Main Terminal opens at Birmingham International Airport.

1987 BCC invites developers to produce proposals for the site of what will later become Brindleyplace, with a planned completion date of 1991. The £23 million proceeds from the sale of the development rights are used by BCC to build the National Indoor Arena (NIA).

1988 Highbury Initiative held at Joseph Chamberlain's former home in Moseley. A wide range of architects, planners and urbanists attend, including Terry Farrell and Will Alsop.

1989 The Prince of Wales condemns the Central Library as 'a place where books are incinerated, not kept'. Planning permission is granted for 56,000 m^2 of office space on the Brindleyplace site.

1990 Sadler's Wells Royal Ballet moves into the Hippodrome and becomes Birmingham Royal Ballet.

1991 The ICC and Symphony Hall are opened by the Queen. The National Indoor Arena opens. Eurohub opens at Birmingham International Airport

1993 The first Birmingham Unitary Development Plan is published. The revamped Victoria Square is unveiled.

1995 The opening of the Water's Edge and the main square mark the completion of the first phase of the Brindleyplace development.

1996 Birmingham acts as a host city for European Football Championship.

1997 The Ikon Gallery reopens in Levitt Bernstein's restored Oozells Street School.

1998 Birmingham hosts the G7 Summit of leading industrialised nations.

1999 Line 1 of the Midland Metro opens. *Regeneration through conservation: Birmingham Conservation Strategy* is published.

2001 Millennium Point opens to the public. The Mailbox opens in the former Royal Mail Sorting Office.

2003 The new Bullring shopping centre opens. The 9th IAAF World Indoor Athletics Championships are held at the NIA. Birmingham bids to become European Capital of Culture 2008. *Distinctly Birmingham*, the local cultural strategy is published.

2004 John McAslan + Partners appointed to redesign Birmingham New Street Station.

2005 Local Development Scheme for Birmingham is published.

2005 Revised Unitary Development Plan is adopted.

2005 MAKE Architects are appointed to design the final phase of the Mailbox development.

2006 Professor Michael Parkinson commissioned to undertake City Centre Masterplan Stage 1 Visioning Study.

2007 Urban Initiatives consortia commissioned to undertake City Centre Masterplan stage 2. Area Investment Prospectuses published.
Housing growth targets for the city set at 50,000 by 2026.

13

01
CITY OF CHANGE

'The town should not, with God's help, know itself.'
Joseph Chamberlain

'Forward'
City of Birmingham civic motto

< J.A. Chatwin's St. Martin's church
contrasts with Future Systems'
Selfridges
CRAIG HOLMES/IMAGES OF BIRMINGHAM

BIRMINGHAM.
from Ravenhurst (neere London road)
on the South-east part of the towne.

Birmingham is a city built on an unshakeable faith in a better and brighter future. There is something in the city's character that causes it to constantly rebuild and reinvent itself, and during much of its history it has been engaged in a relentless cycle of upheaval. To outsiders and indeed many of those who live in the city, it gives an impression of being in a permanent and frenzied state of demolition and regeneration. Alexis de Tocqueville noted during a visit to the town that Birmingham was driven by commerce and a desire to work hard and make money. 'These folk never have a moment to themselves. They work as if they must get rich by the evening, and die the next day', he wrote.[1] As an engine of wealth creation, the bricks and mortar from which Birmingham is made have always had to accept that they are subordinate to the solid Midlands preoccupations of profit and industry. Although the settlement of Birmingham dates back more than a millennium, there is little in the city today to suggest a history of much more than 150 years. Indeed, considering that it achieved its apogee in the late Victorian and Edwardian era, it is remarkable how few buildings even of this period have survived. In Birmingham, the past is never allowed to stand in the way of progress and no street or neighbourhood can ever feel entirely free from the threat of the bulldozer and the wrecking ball. The city's streetscape and even its topography have proven to be remarkably plastic over the centuries, testament to Birmingham's belief in looking forever 'Forward'.

Embracing change is of course a fundamental characteristic of the city and its wider region. The Midlands are the true birthplace of the Industrial Revolution and Birmingham the epicentre of Britain's industrial development, and yet the city achieved success without obvious natural advantages. It is not built on a great river and does not have rich mineral resources. It is a place that has quite literally been built through the enterprise and hard work of its citizens. From aspiring medieval market town, to cradle of the Industrial Revolution and 'workshop of the world', through to its more recent emergence as a world meeting place, Birmingham has demonstrated the sort of entrepreneurial and tenacious spirit of which great cities are made. Aside from being a pioneering industrial centre, Birmingham has also, particularly over the course of the past five decades, become home to a multitude of immigrant communities from around the world, most notably from Ireland, South Asia and the Caribbean. The changes to Birmingham's physical fabric over the past century have in fact been more than matched by equally dramatic changes in its demographics, making Birmingham today one of the most diverse and youthful cities in Europe. Much of the early growth came from people moving to the town from the surrounding region, looking for work and an escape from rural poverty. These early economic migrants were later joined by successive waves of immigration from much further afield. As early as the 1920s, there were Irish, Italian, Cypriot, Polish, Hungarian, Serbian and various Jewish immigrant groups in the city. There is also evidence of a small transient black and Asian population before 1914 — mainly single young men who came to work or study before moving on. Between the two world wars a significant Yemeni community developed in the city and founded what was effectively Birmingham's first mosque. In recent years, the city's *Black Pasts*, *Birmingham Futures Group* has been

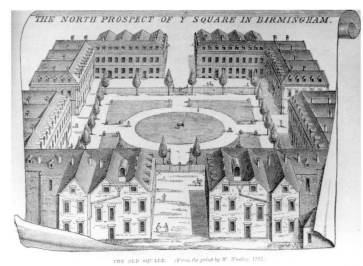

THE OLD SQUARE. (From the print by W. Westley, 1732.)

collecting and recording the incredible and often inspiring stories of its black and Asian communities. Birmingham today is a complex mix of cultures and traditions, and arguably something of a model of a successful multicultural European city. Its history is as much evident in the faces of its citizens as it is in the buildings in which they live and work. It is a history of immigration, reinvention and change.

But despite all its achievements, Birmingham has historically suffered from a peculiar lack of self-confidence and has long been used to receiving derisory comments in the press and the disdain of much of the rest of the country. Queen Victoria is alleged to have requested the blinds of her train carriage be closed whenever she passed the city, a sentiment echoed by the millions of drivers for whom their first and only impression of Birmingham is of passing along the often heavily congested M6 motorway. Given Birmingham's late 20th-century reputation as a concrete desert, it is hard to believe that one visitor's first observations upon arriving in the town back in the 16th century had been: 'I came through a pretty street as ever I entered, into Bermingham towne.'[2] To say that Birmingham has suffered from an image problem in the centuries since then is something of an understatement. Even today, after more than a decade of widely acknowledged progress towards reversing the catastrophic errors of the 1960s and 70s, Birmingham still has a medium-sized mountain to climb in terms of public perceptions. How then did the city arrive where it is today?

The settlement that became modern Birmingham probably dates back at least as far as the 7th century AD. *Bermingcham* receives a mention in the Domesday Book, and in 1156 Peter de Bermingham was granted one of the first market charters in Warwickshire by Henry II. Over the following centuries Birmingham's markets grew to the point where they acted as a regional focus, bringing in livestock traders from as far away as the Welsh Marches. From these humble beginnings on the banks of the River Rea, grew what was to become a centre of enterprise, scientific innovation and political and religious dissent. Birmingham's development over the following centuries was fuelled by the growth of its markets, tanneries, population of economic migrants and eventually its nascent metalworking industries. From the late medieval through to the early modern era, Birmingham seems to have grown steadily in influence within the region. William Camden noted how the place was 'swarming with inhabitants and echoing with the noise of anvils'[3] when he passed through in 1563. It was not long afterwards that the town became noted for its arms trade, having supplied the Parliamentary side during the Civil War, and by the beginning of the 18th century Birmingham had surpassed Coventry to become the largest town in Warwickshire.

It was during the 18th century that Birmingham went through its first golden era. The growing success of its iron, steel and brass goods was accompanied by an emerging class of wealthy entrepreneurs and professionals desiring new residences that suited their improved and elevated status. The town grew at an unprecedented rate, with developments such as the Square, Birmingham's first formally planned set-piece development, setting new standards in urban design.[4]

17

The local economy was given a further boost by the growing canal network that by the end of the century had made Birmingham accessible from most parts of the country. Within this economic and engineering revolution, Birmingham was also witnessing the stirrings of its own philosophical Enlightenment. Foremost amongst the informal scientific groupings that proliferated at the time was the town's Lunar Society, which met at local industrialist Matthew Boulton's house at the full moon of each month. Counting James Watt, Josiah Wedgwood and the Unitarian preacher and radical Joseph Priestley amongst its members, it is not surprising that ten of the Lunar Society went on to become Fellows of the Royal Society. Priestley described the ambitions of the society as follows:

We had nothing to do with the religious or political principles of each other. We were united by a common love of Science, which we thought sufficient to bring together persons of all distinctions, Christians, Jews, Mohametans, and Heathens, Monarchists and Republicans.[5]

Priestley's view of a tolerant and mutually respectful society was not, however, shared by all the citizens of the town. In the late 1700s, Priestley's sympathy for the French Revolution was well known and his house was attacked by a drunken mob and virtually destroyed. The 'Priestley Riots' have become part of Birmingham legend and a salutary reminder that the town was not always as liberal minded as it is today. Priestley left Birmingham for the recently founded United States of America, seeking the intellectual toleration that he had failed to find at home.

But enlightenment and reform never entirely disappeared from the Birmingham landscape. The main tools of reform in the early years of transition from Midlands market town to regional capital were the Improvement Acts. There were a series of five Improvement Acts for Birmingham between 1769 and 1828, each one designed specifically to deal with a particular area of the town's upkeep. In the process of introducing this patchwork of legislation, parliament gradually eroded the jurisdiction of the manorial court and parish.[6] The street commissioners, who were established by these acts, gradually accumulated a growing number of those duties with which we might associate modern local government, such as responsibility for the markets and night watchmen. In 1807 the commissioners opened their own offices on Moor Street, a small but symbolic step towards the establishment of a local government bureaucracy. The fifth Act of 1828 ushered in the last and most active period in the history of the commissioners, during which they built Charles Edge's market hall and commissioned Hansom and Welch's much-loved Town Hall. The street commissioners' responsibilities finally passed to the new town council in 1851, which for many decades was run by a 'shopkeeper cabal'[7] of relatively

modest ambitions. Indeed, Birmingham's transition from prosperous but unambitious provincial town to a model of 19th-century civic governance was sometimes slow and often hampered by reactionary local dignitaries, with many of the improvements being driven by legislation from Westminster.

It was not really until Joseph Chamberlain became mayor in 1873 that the scale of the council's ambitions finally began to befit those of a place the size of Birmingham. When Chamberlain originally arrived from London in 1854, there were no free schools, art galleries, libraries or parks. While Manchester and Glasgow had pioneered reform in healthcare and education, Birmingham, still only a town, showed no such inclinations. Like many of his contemporaries, Chamberlain originally came to Birmingham in search of a career in industry, attracted by its reputation for enterprise and opportunity. But he was also a Liberal with a strong Christian faith, and was equally drawn to the city's Nonconformist religion and radical politics. He railed against what he saw as the hypocrisy of progressive men who became reactionary upon acquiring wealth and influence, and was determined that if he were to achieve success it would not be at the expense of his morals or sense of civic obligation. He became a disciple of the Birmingham preacher George Dawson's 'Civic Gospel', which combined evangelical zeal with a belief in the redemptive power of the well-governed city, and on becoming mayor Chamberlain laid out his clear and simple vision: 'The town should not, with God's help, know itself'.[8] Having initially been reluctant to extend its field of influence, under Chamberlain the council became aggressively expansionist, municipalising water and forging ahead in education reform. His period as mayor, and the seven decades of sensibly managed prosperity that they ushered in, probably represent the era in which Birmingham was most confident and certain of its own place in the world. In 1889 the town finally became a city, and within a decade work had begun on a new university in Edgbaston. It was a time when Birmingham could be referred to without irony in the American *Harper's Monthly* as the 'The best-governed city in the world'.[9] As a civic leader, Chamberlain set standards in public office that Birmingham had never previously expected or aspired to. He was driven, ambitious and a visionary. He transformed not only the physical character of the town, ploughing grand boulevards such as Corporation Street through decrepit slums, but also its public services, using the proceeds from Birmingham's municipalised utilities to subsidise cutting-edge reforms in the arts and education. Building upon the vision of George Dawson, and aided by countless other like-minded men and women, Chamberlain helped to create a model of efficient, benevolent and enterprising civic governance that has had a lasting impact around the world.

Between 1891 and 1911, Birmingham's population overtook that of Glasgow to make it the UK's second largest city after London.[10] Much of this growth was brought about by the merger of surrounding districts with the city. The Greater Birmingham Act of 1911 was a key moment in the city's history, as areas such as Aston, Handsworth and King's Norton were brought within its boundaries. Some of the most significant changes in the physical fabric of the city during the late 19th and early 20th centuries took place in these growing suburbs. Many of the small and medium-sized firms that had characterised Birmingham's early industrial development began to move out of the centre in search of space to expand. As early as 1879, George Cadbury had begun development of a model village for his chocolate-factory workers just south of Birmingham in a rural area he named 'Bournville'. Run according to Quaker principles, in line

with the Cadbury family's own beliefs, the Bournville estate provided schools and recreational facilities for workers and residents. To this day, no alcohol is permitted for sale on the estate. This early garden suburb was eventually subsumed into the city itself and handed over by the Cadbury family to the control of the Bournville Village Trust. With much of the best design overseen by its chief architect, William Alexander Harvey, Bournville set a high standard for suburban development within Birmingham and was to be influential in creating a model for both private and social housing over many decades.

In 1901, a series of articles by J. Cuming Walters, entitled 'Scenes in Slumland' and describing the conditions in Birmingham's deprived inner-city neighbourhoods, were published in the *Birmingham Daily Gazette*. They provoked a public outcry, and soon afterwards a new council housing committee was formed with the specific task of bringing about improvements in the city's new suburbs and estates. The committee's first chairman, John Sutton Nettlefold, drew on a wide range of influences, including a tour of German housing projects and the ideas of the Manchester reformer T. C. Horsfall, to develop a distinctive and lasting vision of how Birmingham should plan its future expansion. Clearly also inspired by Bournville and the Garden Suburb movement, he believed that the most appropriate role for local authorities was not in actually building houses, but in laying out streets and parks, with the plots of land then left to private developers, self-help groups and individuals to develop. Nettlefold stated:

> We cannot hope to make Birmingham into a Garden City, although something can be done towards that end, but we can, if we will, create Garden Suburbs around Birmingham. [11]

Nettlefold's beliefs were highly influential in the development of the city, and contributed towards the abundance of high-quality suburbs. Birmingham was fortunate at this time to have plentiful amounts of land available for residential development, and with Nettlefold's instinctive belief in low-rise housing a critical decision was made that the city would pursue a model of development that was diffuse and sprawling. As a consequence, the prevailing character of most of Birmingham's residential neighbourhoods from 1900 to 1939 is leafy, spacious and suburban. Many of them remain almost unchanged and there are countless suburban roads in Birmingham that stand as reminders of Nettlefold's vision, with wide central reservations, grass verges and numerous trees.

The city centre, by contrast, was to develop in a very different way. Despite plans for a major new civic centre along Broad Street in the 1930s, the main Victorian core survived relatively intact until the Blitz. During the four decades that followed the Second World War, much damage was done to Britain's towns and cities, and while never renowned for its beauty Birmingham suffered even more than most. With its motto of 'Forward' and the example set by Joseph Chamberlain, it is

almost as if successive council administrations felt the need to surpass the visionary plans of the previous generation in their vastness and ambition. The post-war politicians were part of a generation that saw their role as literally building a better Britain. In Birmingham this was exemplified by an abiding love affair with the American urban model, exemplified by an emphasis on gyratory roads and commercially driven redevelopment such as the disastrous Bullring shopping mall. A typical attitude during the 1970s was expressed by Clive Wilkinson, the Labour leader of the council at the time the Victorian wholesale markets were demolished: 'I would absolutely agree that we rushed the demolition of the old market, and I am not apologising for it.'[12] In Birmingham, this zealousness for demolition and rebuilding was taken further than in almost any other major British city. By the early 1970s, Birmingham had more tower blocks than any other local authority in the country and an extremely expensive inner-city gyratory system – the Inner Ring Road. Hundreds of acres of Victorian housing, only some of which were truly slums, had been swept away, with communities uprooted and rehoused in new council estates. The pace of this change was unbelievably fast, and more often than not, it did not involve consultation with the people it affected most – the citizens of Birmingham. Newspaper headlines from the 1960s onwards record a growing tide of resentment at the social and psychological damage caused by the well-intentioned but often disastrously implemented rehousing projects. A report by the Department of the Environment in 1975 claimed that bulldozers had 'blighted vast acreages' of Birmingham and set the scene for a host of social problems. 'Comprehensive redevelopment has produced incalculable psychological stress, and created an atmosphere in which vandalism is rife', the report went on to say.[13] The end result across the city was nearly a thousand often poorly constructed system-built tower blocks. The combination of unremittingly mediocre architecture and an apparent obsession with road building set the scene for decades of ridicule as Birmingham turned itself into the archetypal concrete jungle – parodied as a car-obsessed city of drab pedestrian underpasses and disorientating roundabouts.

The key figure behind many of the major post-war planning decisions was neither a planner nor an architect, but Herbert Manzoni, the City Engineer. The notorious Inner Ring Road, originally envisaged as a series of tree-lined avenues in William Haywood's 1918 publication *The Development of Birmingham*, became in the hands of Herbert Manzoni an urban motorway – the 'concrete collar' that would stifle growth, discourage shoppers and create an image of a city gone car- and concrete-mad. Manzoni outlined his views on Birmingham as follows:

23

I have never been very certain as to the value of tangible links with the past. They are often more sentimental than valuable... As to Birmingham's buildings, there is little of real worth in our architecture. Its replacement should be an improvement, provided we keep a few monuments as museum pieces to past ages... As for future generations, I think they will be better occupied in applying their thoughts and energies to forging ahead, rather than looking backward.[14]

The damage wreaked upon the city during this period was immense, and notorious acts of architectural vandalism have continued right up to the present day. The General Post Office building on Hill Street was knocked down in 1973, as was the old Lucas Factory on Great King Street in 1994. One of the greatest acts of destruction, during what might be described as the 'Sacking of Birmingham', was the demolition of Martin and Chamberlain's old Central Library. This much-admired building was torn down in 1974 not to make way for the new library, which was already under construction next door, but to allow for the final sections of the Inner Ring Road. The public campaign against demolition was spearheaded by Joe Holyoak, an architect and academic who has gone on to play an influential role in the evolving attitudes to planning within the city. Although the campaign failed and the old library was needlessly demolished, the resulting controversy contributed to a gradual reassessment of Birmingham's attitude towards old buildings and its urban fabric in general. It would be going too far to say that Birmingham became a convert to architectural conservation, but for a time the pace of destruction slackened. In the following decades, as Birmingham's and the UK's economic fortunes slowly recovered, the pressure to redevelop would return, raising unresolved questions of how the city should manage and adapt to massive change.

NOTES

[1] Quoted in Chris Upton, *A History of Birmingham*, Phillimore, Chichester, 1993, p. 42.

[2] Quoted in Chris Upton, *A History of Birmingham*, Phillimore, Chichester, 1993, p. 12.

[3] Quoted in Chris Upton, *A History of Birmingham*, Phillimore, Chichester, 1993, p. 12.

[4] Joseph McKenna, *Birmingham: The Building of a City*, Tempus, Stroud, 2005, pp. 25–6.

[5] Quoted in Jenny Uglow, *The Lunar Men*, Faber and Faber, London, 2002, p. xiv.

[6] Gordon E. Cherry, *Birmingham: A Study in Geography, History and Planning*, John Wiley & Sons, Chichester, 1994, p. 53.

[7] Tristram Hunt, *Building Jerusalem*, Weidenfeld & Nicolson, London, 2004, p. 239.

[8] Joseph Chamberlain, quoted in Conrad Gill and Charles Grant Robertson, *A Short History of Birmingham*, City of Birmingham Information Bureau, Birmingham, 1938, p. 58.

[9] J. Ralph, *Harper's Monthly Magazine*, quoted in Joseph McKenna, *Birmingham: The Building of a City*, Tempus, Stroud, 2005, p. 66.

[10] Joseph McKenna, *Birmingham: The Building of a City*, Tempus, Stroud, 2005, p. 89.

[11] Quoted in Gordon E. Cherry, *The Politics of Town Planning*, Longman, Harlow, 1982, p. 18.

[12] *Evening Mail*, 3 May 1974.

[13] *Birmingham Mail*, 13 August 1975.

[14] Quoted in Andy Foster, *Birmingham*, Yale University Press, London, 2005, p. 197.

02
FROM A CITY OF ROUNDABOUTS TO A CITY OF SQUARES

Unlike the North of England, the Midlands continued as an economic and industrial powerhouse well into the 1970s and Birmingham remained relatively wealthy and successful. Throughout the 1970s the city continued to see itself as much closer to the more affluent Southeast than the declining North of England, but by the early 1980s the collapse in manufacturing had begun to necessitate a fundamental change of direction.

During the course of numerous recessions in the period from 1971 to 1987, Birmingham lost 191,000 jobs, or 29 per cent of all its employment, mainly in manufacturing. Having lost so much of the industry that had given the city its identity and self-confidence, the Handsworth riots of 1985 then underlined how inadequately the economic and demographic change was being handled. In its rush to modernise during the post-war years and impress the world with its commitment to 'progress', Birmingham had in actual fact inflicted massive physical and psychological trauma upon itself. The city's robust Victorian urban fabric had been carved up and replaced not by a utopia, but by a dysfunctional terrain of urban motorways, concrete underpasses and undistinguished architectural tat. Birmingham's diverse immigrant communities found themselves increasingly isolated within a ring of decrepit and decaying inner-city neighbourhoods. Under the guise of modernisation, Birmingham had in actual fact prostrated itself before a tide of rash and thoughtless redevelopment.

A policy of seeing any development as a good development had blinded the city's leaders to the mediocrity of the urban environment they were creating. Most disastrous of all had been the construction of the Inner Ring Road, which had been literally bulldozed through the city, leaving the fringes of its centre looking devastated and deserted. The planners had banished countless people from living in the actual city centre, with entire neighbourhoods demolished and their inhabitants relocated to distant council estates. Local and national economic instability, combined with the shattering blow inflicted by the 1974 IRA pub bombings, had left the city centre in a seemingly irreversible spiral of decline. By the mid-1980s, central Birmingham was a diesel-choked, economic wasteland. Following this catastrophic collapse, the city's leaders were finally forced to confront the need for fundamental change in the city's economy and physical fabric. As the wealth and then the self-confidence began to evaporate, Birmingham realised that it had to adapt to a changed landscape in which manufacturing would increasingly take a back seat to the service industries. The city's regeneration has therefore largely been driven by economic necessity rather than civic idealism. The key plank in this re-branding exercise was to be the reinvention of Birmingham as a conference and exhibition city. The city had made its first significant move into the exhibition trade with the National Exhibition Centre in 1976, but although hugely successful[1] the NEC was technically outside Birmingham on the rural fringes of the city. What the council wanted to achieve, was a transformation of the city centre itself – a project that would inject new economic life and transform perceptions.

Historically, Birmingham has often looked across the Atlantic for its role models, and in the 1980s the city's leaders turned their attentions to Baltimore, which had reinvented itself as a convention destination in the United States. Baltimore was an East-Coast port that had experienced serious industrial and population decline, but which had responded to these challenges by opening the Baltimore Convention Centre in 1979, the 'festival marketplace' Harbourplace development in 1980 and the Baltimore National Aquarium in 1981. This was almost precisely the model that was later to be adopted in Birmingham during the 1980s and 1990s. As will be seen, the International Convention Centre, Brindleyplace and the National Sealife Centre are all directly related to these earlier developments, built a decade earlier on the other side of the Atlantic. The Birmingham Convention Centre project began formally in 1984, when the city council whittled down a shortlist of six architectural practices, controversially rejecting Richard Rogers in order to appoint the combined team of Percy Thomas Partnership and RHWL. The project was a massive undertaking, and typical of the city's historic tendency towards big and ambitious projects. Eleven separate conference and exhibition

< Just some of the
hundreds of tower
blocks built in
Birmingham during the
1960s and 70s
PAUL WARD/IMAGES OF
BIRMINGHAM

∨ Chamberlain Square with
the Museum and Art
Gallery and the Town Hall
PAUL WARD/IMAGES OF
BIRMINGHAM

∨ A bustling pedestrianised
New Street
CRAIG HOLMES/IMAGES OF
BIRMINGHAM

∨ The International Convention Centre
CRAIG HOLMES/IMAGES OF BIRMINGHAM

halls were required, as well as a world-class concert hall for the City of Birmingham Symphony Orchestra and its young conductor, Simon Rattle. In preparation, a large swathe of Broad Street was cleared of buildings, with only a handful of existing structures retained. At a time when central government funding for such projects was practically non-existent, Birmingham's decision to push ahead with a £126 million capital project was bold to say the least. Undeterred, the city council set about sourcing the money from wherever it could, including the European Community and, most notoriously, the city's education budget. Unsurprisingly, the project raised political hackles amongst some Labour traditionalists and was condemned as elitist and a misappropriation of funds. However, like the NEC before it, the ICC project survived thanks to strong support amongst the leadership of both main political parties on the council, most notably from the then leader Dick Knowles.[2] The ICC was opened by the Queen in 1991, with the 1992 EC Summit being one of the first major events to be held there. Symphony Hall in particular was hailed as a triumph and was immediately recognised as being amongst the best concert halls in the world.

The urgent need to create a city centre that could accommodate the anticipated thousands of convention delegates had also necessitated a wider rethink of the council's planning strategy. In March 1988 an event took place at Joseph Chamberlain's old house, Highbury Hall in Moseley, which would help change Birmingham for ever. The City Centre Challenge Symposium, or 'Highbury Initiative' as the event was soon dubbed, has come to symbolise a defining moment in the history of Birmingham, marking the start of a radically new approach to urban design within the city. Although the council had already begun to identify some of the key issues with its own City Centre Strategy document in 1987, the symposium was a recognition of the need to bring the best national and international expertise to bear on some complex and challenging problems. Present at the event were leading policy-makers, developers and architects, including Will Alsop and Terry Farrell. Many of them were from outside the city and brought with them a vital critical distance. Their task was to challenge the existing status quo and identify the key objectives that should drive the city's future approaches to urban design and development. What the Highbury Initiative went on to establish was the need to improve perceptions of the city through dramatic improvements to the public realm. Birmingham urgently needed to break down the barrier created by the Inner Ring Road and create attractive streets and squares, in which people would be engaged and stimulated and around which businesses would be keen to invest. The symposium identified that public and private partnerships had been a key factor in successful city-centre regeneration projects around the world, from Baltimore to Barcelona, and helped establish this model as a central element of Birmingham's new vision. It also recognised that it was often incumbent upon the public sector to take the lead and show the necessary confidence and commitment before the private sector became fully involved. The establishment of long-term relationships between the public and private sector was therefore identified as a key early priority for the city council and the business community.

The most enduring and significant outputs from the Highbury Initiative were the 'Hilderbrandt' and 'Birmingham Urban Design Study' reports. Don Hilderbrandt was a US urban designer who had been a delegate at the Highbury Initiative and was invited to produce a report that would point the way forward for the city's pedestrianisation agenda. His report, published in September 1988, was to be highly influential in guiding change within the city centre over the next two decades. It established a set of clear themes, including accessibility, legibility, architecture and urban fabric. The report also recommended reintroducing conventional surface-level crossings along the Inner Ring Road and

redirecting through-traffic to the Middle Ring Road. Additionally, it identified a series of key spaces around the city centre that needed to be upgraded and integrated into a network of pedestrian routes across the city. In many ways, the Hilderbrandt Report was a blueprint for every major alteration to the public realm that was to take place in Birmingham over the next 20 years. These included raising Old Square, lowering Smallbrook Queensway, and the restoration of a visual link between New Street and St Martin's Church. Looking at the document today, it is clear that, with the exception of a city centre light-rail system, every significant objective has been achieved. At the time, however, it was far from certain that these changes would come about. The most lasting legacy of this period of change has been the pedestrianisation of the city centre and the radical overhaul of the city's public realm. The first manifestation of this new approach was Centenary Square, which was conceived as a grand public space and foreground to the new Convention Centre. Centenary Square also set a new precedent for commissioning public art as part of all major projects within the city. The square itself was designed by the city's own Landscape Group, in collaboration with the artist Tess Jaray. Sculptures by Tom Lomax and, most controversially, Raymond Mason's 'Forward' sculpture placed Birmingham at the forefront of the public-art debate within the UK. It is difficult to appreciate today just how radical and far-sighted this scheme was, but Centenary Square represented a huge leap forward for Birmingham as a city. For the first time in years, it could genuinely be said to be amongst the most cutting-edge and forward-looking cities in the country. Centenary Square was followed by the pedestrianisation of New Street and the complete redesign of Victoria Square. Like its predecessor, Victoria Square is conceived as a traditional grand civic space, with fountains, statuary and the use of stone, brick and elegant plane trees. The formal classicism of the square is subtly balanced by the artworks, sculpted by Indian-born Royal Academician Dhruva Mistry, who depicts mythical beasts that make clear references to both classical European and Eastern art. In many ways, the square represents the most ambitious and successful attempt in the built environment at a creative expression of Birmingham's cultural and ethnic diversity.

Another key recommendation of the Highbury Initiative was that the city should nurture its distinct inner-city neighbourhoods, accentuating and building upon their unique characteristics. One of these distinctive areas was the Jewellery Quarter. Located just north of Birmingham city centre, in Hockley, the Jewellery Quarter is a relatively unchanged slice of 19th-century industrial Birmingham. It has been a focus for the jewellery trade for around 200 years, and remains one of the most important centres of jewellery manufacture in Europe. In the post-war years there were plans for wholesale redevelopment with 'flatted factories' – high-rise industrial buildings, surrounded by open space. Fortunately, only a small area was cleared before a growing appreciation of the quarter's distinct qualities put paid to the plans. As early as 1971, three small Conservation Areas had been created, and in 2002 English Heritage finally carried out a complete appraisal of the area, cataloguing its unique architectural and industrial heritage. Today, the Jewellery Quarter has developed a thriving retail sector and growing tourist industry. The Museum of the Jewellery Quarter, a former abandoned workshop that was later bought by the city council and turned into a museum, is a popular attraction. This was followed in 1989 by Derek Latham Architects' conversion of a nearby block of disused workshops on the corner of Spencer Street and Hockley Street into 65 rentable units for the Duchy of Cornwall. The Jewellery Business Centre on Spencer Street is now home to dozens of small businesses, while the centre's distinctive gates, by Michael Johnson, have become something of a local landmark. In line with the Hilderbrandt Report, the council has

∧ Oozells Square, Brindleyplace
CRAIG HOLMES/IMAGES OF BIRMINGHAM

pursued a deliberate policy of trying to preserve the unique character of this and other historic inner-city areas. The past decade has seen strong pressure for increased residential development in and around the Jewellery Quarter, and Bryant Priest Newman have responded admirably to the challenge with their Albion Square and Octohedron developments. The question remains as how best to balance the demand for new housing with the survival of the jewellery industry, but at least the protection of the area's essential architectural character is now assured.

Following from its huge success, and as the city council had hoped, the Convention Centre was to become the epicentre of a wave of regeneration that would totally transform the surrounding area. In 1987, while the ICC took shape, the council drew up the development brief for what would become Brindleyplace. This large block of land to the west of the Convention Centre was sold in a competitive bidding process, with the proceeds going towards the construction of the proposed National Indoor Arena. The model for this huge development was Baltimore's Festival Marketplace, and the winning bidder for the project was an alliance of three companies: Merlin, Shearwater and Laing.[3] Running the project was Alan Chatham, who would go on to become a key figure in the city's regeneration over the coming decades. Chatham saw Brindleyplace through an extremely difficult period in which the scheme changed ownership, finally being taken on by Argent in 1993 just as the UK economy was pulling out of another deep recession. During this time, the original masterplan was scrapped in favour of a new design by Terry Farrell Partnership. In line with changing attitudes to urban design and the conclusions of the Highbury Initiative, the Farrell masterplan rejected single mega-structures in favour of traditional urban blocks, defined by streets and squares. For the city council and its then newly appointed Director of Planning and Architecture Les Sparks, one of the key objectives for Brindleyplace was to demonstrate that commercial housing development could work in the city centre. For decades the council had been discouraging housing in the central core, but now this policy was about to be dramatically reversed. Regular meetings were held between the design team and the planning authority, helping to ensure that the overall scheme fitted well with the recommendations of the Hilderbrandt and BUDS reports. A coherent set of design guidelines were established, within which various architects could design distinct buildings that still worked together to create a coherent whole. Former Farrell partner John Chatwin went on to develop the masterplan as-built and, unlike previous developments in the city, a high priority was attached to the quality of the public realm and the architecture. In an innovative move, the central square, by Townshend Landscape, was actually built before any of the surrounding buildings. This emphasis on quality spaces and 'sense of place' was a key part of the Brindleyplace philosophy. From the very start there was a notion that Brindleyplace was a destination in itself, and this was underlined by Argent's commitment to a series of arts events that took place within the central square even as the surrounding office buildings were coming out of the ground.

The buildings themselves have been designed by a range of like-minded practices, whose work is clearly distinct but complementary, such as Allies and Morrison, Porphyrios Associates and Stanton Williams. All the buildings on the main square incorporate the same tripartite façade composition, with a common cornice line and similarly scaled arcades, giving the scheme a rare coherency and legibility. This common language has been interpreted freely enough by the various practices to ensure that there is still a strong individual character running through each of the buildings. The cultural linchpin of the scheme is Levitt Bernstein's refurbished school building for the Ikon Gallery, while the public spaces are enlivened with artworks by Miles Davies and, most successfully, Paul de Monchaux in Oozells Square. A

< The National Indoor
Arena
CRAIG HOLMES/IMAGES OF
BIRMINGHAM

∧ Baltimore Convention Centre
BALTIMORE AREA CONVENTION &
VISITORS ASSOCIATION

∧ The International
Convention Centre
CRAIG HOLMES/IMAGES OF
BIRMINGHAM

∨ New lighting on the underside of the A38
flyover, commissioned by the Mailbox
CRAIG HOLMES/IMAGES OF BIRMINGHAM

∧ CZWG's cafe at
Brindleyplace
CRAIG HOLMES/IMAGES OF
BIRMINGHAM

mix of architecture and public art, Piers Gough's jewel-like café acts as a visual focus for the entire development with its axial position at the heart of the main square. Unsurprisingly, Brindleyplace has become a national model for urban design. It incorporates many of the key urban design ideas that had been emerging internationally over the previous two decades, and implements them with great success. The masterplan and architecture set new standards for commercial developments within the city. Crucially, Crosby Homes' Symphony Court development set a precedent for new privately owned housing within the city centre. It was no surprise that when Alan Chatham left Argent and Brindleyplace to establish his own company he took with him the same passion for good architecture, mixed uses and vibrant new urban spaces. His next project, the Mailbox, is a testament to his own personal vision and boldness as a developer.

Running almost in parallel with the development of the Convention Centre and Brindleyplace was the saga of the city's other key major city-centre project – the redevelopment of the unloved 1960s Bullring Shopping Centre. In decline almost from the moment it opened, by the 1980s the Bullring was a partially let embarrassment for the city. Although originally hailed as ground-breaking, being one of the first American-style indoor shopping malls in Europe, the Bullring was architecturally undistinguished and incredibly difficult to navigate. Most crucially, it completely blocked all visual connections with Digbeth, of which the original Bull Ring marketplace had been a natural extension. Old photographs illustrate how the city once sloped steeply from the junction of New Street and High Street down to the old medieval heart of the town around St Martin's Church, while the 1960s redevelopment, which straddled the Inner Ring Road, formed a huge barrier to movement, effectively cutting off the south of the city centre. Beginning in 1987, various developers and architects put forward a series of different proposals that varied in their urban design and architectural merits but which always retained the concept of a single monolithic shopping centre. At one point local campaign group Birmingham for People proposed an alternative scheme that incorporated mixed-uses and traditional urban blocks. The designs, drawn up by Joe Holyoak, attempted to demonstrate that the redevelopment could accommodate both housing and commercial retail space, a concept that was unfortunately never adopted. Having been repeatedly delayed due to recession and changes in ownership, the Bullring redevelopment was finally brought to fruition by the Birmingham Alliance[4] in 2003. Although the project as realised did not meet all of the campaigners' demands there were significant concessions, with the final scheme allowing for the complete removal of part of the Inner Ring Road. Birmingham for People's biggest success was in convincing the developers to restore the crucial visual and pedestrian link with St Martin's Church, thanks to which Digbeth once again feels like an extension of the city centre.

The new Bullring shopping centre is, of course, best known for the Selfridges department store that has given the city its first globally recognisable landmark building. Designed by Future Systems, its curvaceous profile and unmistakable silver discs have become synonymous with Birmingham. Few buildings ever achieve this ubiquity, and few other cities in the UK are capable of being recognised by a single piece of architecture. Selfridges has had a mixed response within the city, with many locals finding it a difficult building to appreciate. What is undeniable, however, is the extent to which it has helped change outside perceptions of the city and how it is evolving. In a 2006 survey, Selfridges was ranked amongst the top ten UK landmarks that tourists visiting the country wanted to see and photograph.[5] Thanks to Selfridges, the city now has a profile on the global architectural scene that it has probably never had before. People now come to Birmingham almost for the sole purpose of seeing some architecture – surely a first.

As well as the huge prestige building projects, Birmingham has also been carefully cultivating its cultural scene. The Ikon Gallery, founded in 1963, has long been at the forefront of contemporary art within the city and is today recognised as one of the leading visual arts organisations in Europe. The city's own Museum and Art Gallery has seen significant expansions, with Stanton Williams's stunning Gas Hall and the adjacent Water Hall by Associated Architects. In 2002,

> A memorial
to Motor City
- Glenn Howell's
wall of crushed
cars at the
Custard Factory
CRAIG HOLMES/IMAGES
OF BIRMINGHAM

^ Gibb Street, the
Custard Factory
CRAIG HOLMES/IMAGES
OF BIRMINGHAM

the city made a strong and concerted bid to become European Capital of Culture 2008. Although Liverpool was the eventual winner, Birmingham's innovative bid, produced in cooperation with the wider region, helped kick-start a more far-reaching cultural agenda within the city. It also added to a growing realisation that Birmingham has an important role as an economic and cultural powerhouse for the region. Birmingham has had a particularly strong track record as a city of music, dating back to the Triennial Music Festival which began in 1778 and continued up until the First World War.[6] The City of Birmingham Symphony Orchestra, particularly during the conductorship of Simon Rattle, has come to be regarded as amongst the finest in the world. But Birmingham is of course home to a multitude of other musical traditions. Not least of these is bhangra, a hybrid of traditional North Indian music and western pop influences, for which Birmingham is a key international centre of both production and consumption. This rich heritage was recognised when Birmingham was pronounced UK City of Music in 1992. The success continues across myriad different organisations and venues. Since its relocation from Sadler's Wells, The Birmingham Royal Ballet continues to grow in prestige and reputation from its base at the city's refurbished Hippodrome, and has since helped attract other dance-related organisations to the city, including the Elmhurst Dance School in Edgbaston. It is also primarily through culture that Birmingham has made the biggest efforts to embrace its growing diversity. Glenn Howells Architects' Custard Factory in Digbeth is a complex of refurbished industrial buildings and new insertions that caters for a huge mixture of artists, designers and other assorted creative industries. Associated Architects' Drum in Aston is a venue specifically built for the promotion of Afro-Caribbean and Asian arts, and has enjoyed significant success since it opened in 2002. Elsewhere, existing organisations have consolidated years of community work by expanding into new premises. The Afro-Caribbean Millennium Centre on Dudley Road has been helping local people explore their cultural and vocational horizons for many years. In 2004, the organisation moved into new purpose-built premises designed by Birmingham-based D5 Architects.

Birmingham's regeneration began in the city centre and continues to be heavily focused on this relatively small area. However, as the 1990s progressed there were growing demands that the rest of the city should receive more attention. The problem centred on the fact that the rejuvenated city centre was perceived as catering primarily for young professionals, while the wider demographic was being ignored. In particular, the growth in city-centre living from the mid-1990s onwards was focused almost entirely on the buy-to-let market, with little in the way of new affordable housing to cater for families or the elderly. Essentially, there appeared to be a danger of creating a city centre that was exclusively young, childless and affluent, while the older and more demographically diverse residential areas had to deal with relative neglect. Two major schemes were initiated in the 1990s that would begin to address this imbalance, and although many problems remain, the city has now shown that it is capable of far more than just prestige city-centre regeneration. One of these success stories has been the transformation of Castle Vale, on the eastern outskirts of the city. This huge post-war development, built on the site of a former airfield, had by the early 1990s developed all the hallmarks of a failed estate. Tower blocks dominated an area that had become bedevilled by crime, unemployment and

35

a decaying environment. The first sign that things might change came in 1991, when the Labour city council put aside its political differences with the Conservative government and entered into talks about how to improve the estate. In 1993, it was announced that Castle Vale would be one of six experimental Housing Action Trusts around the country. By 1996, £205 million[7] had been secured towards the long-term renewal of the area and Hunt Thompson Associates had established the masterplan that would guide the physical regeneration of the estate over the next six years. This allowed for phased demolition of decrepit housing and the unloved Castle Vale Shopping Centre, to be replaced by new residential accommodation and a new retail centre. Elsewhere, existing low-rise housing was renovated and improved. The final, and architecturally most successful, element of the HAT redevelopment came with Associated Architects' masterplan for the estate's secondary shopping centre, Reed Square. While some of what had been built before was rather timid, Reed Square provides the area with a centre that has a real urban presence and offers a 'destination' to which people actually want to travel. A new library, community college and retail units provide a physical and communal focus for the entire estate. Although the Castle Vale HAT was largely disappointing as an architectural project, by employing an innovative mix of public and private finance, with strong community involvement, it did suggest a new direction in which future estate-renewal projects could go.

By partly removing control of housing stock from the city council and introducing a greater mixture of tenants and owner-occupiers, Castle Vale established a precedent that has now been followed elsewhere in the city – most notably in the former Lee Bank estate, south of the city centre. This area, once as notorious as Castle Vale, was identified for massive renewal in the late 1990s and is now in the process of being rebuilt as 'Park Central'. Part of the much larger Attwood Green regeneration initiative, Park Central is a joint venture between Crest Nicholson, Optima Housing Association and Birmingham City Council. As at Castle Vale, there was initially scepticism within some quarters of the ruling Labour group on the council regarding any proposal to transfer more housing stock out of its control. However, in the face of continued decline on the estate and pressure from tenants who were unimpressed with the council's performance, the Labour group finally consented to the transferral of housing stock to Optima Community Association, which was backed by £46 million of government funding as part of the Estates Renewal Challenge Fund.[8] In 2000, Gardner Stewart Architects won a competition for a new masterplan, placing a strong emphasis on high-quality urban design and public spaces. The masterplan focuses on a 7-acre park and, as at Castle Vale, included both the demolition and refurbishment of some existing buildings. To a greater extent than at Castle Vale, the Park Central redevelopment has been driven by a coherent and unifying approach to its architecture. The close proximity to the city centre has also benefited the project, making the commercial elements of the scheme viable in a way that would not have been possible on the outskirts of the city. Underlying the new housing is a philosophy of being 'tenure blind', with housing-association tenants and owner-occupiers mixed together across the development. Architecturally, Park Central has a clear and consistent approach to massing and materials that give it a strong sense of place, and it has already won numerous regeneration awards. With completion scheduled for 2012, Park Central is still far from finished, but the signs are that it will be one of the most sophisticated regeneration projects the city has seen.

The success of projects such as Park Central is a vindication of the radical steps taken to break the 'concrete collar' of the Inner Ring Road in the period from the late 1980s to the present day. Without this process, city-centre growth and expansion would have been impossible. By the start of the new millennium, the momentum towards regeneration in every direction was unstoppable. There do, however, remain serious impediments to this process. Although huge progress has been made towards downgrading the Inner Ring Road, it remains a major barrier to movement along Great Charles Street and Bristol Street, and around Paradise Circus. As the next chapter will demonstrate, there are plans afoot to deal with many of these issues, but they illustrate how urban-design mistakes made decades ago can linger on for generations.

Even in recent decades, good urban design and architecture has often been sadly absent outside of the city centre. As already mentioned, regeneration has necessarily been focused on the commercial heart of the city, and while there has been investment elsewhere, such as at Castle Vale, this has rarely produced buildings or spaces to compare to those in the city centre. The University of Birmingham, which was once responsible for commissioning some of the city's best

^ Sculpture by
Dhruva Mistry,
Victoria Square
CRAIG HOLMES/IMAGES
OF BIRMINGHAM

modern architecture, has built little of quality for several decades. Berman Guedes Stretton's National NMR Facility is a welcome but rare exception, although the university's appointment of MacCormac Jamieson Pritchard to devise the first comprehensive masterplan for the campus since Casson and Conder in the 1960s suggests that things may be about to improve. In contrast, the University of Central England has commissioned a series of excellent buildings from Associated Architects over the last two decades, including several critically acclaimed refurbishments for the Birmingham Institute of Art and Design as well as the new Westbourne Campus for the Faculty of Health. Elsewhere, there are a few gems scattered throughout the inner suburbs and outlying areas of the city, notably Niall Philips's new visitor centre and gallery at Blakesley Hall in Yardley and Bryant Priest Newman's and David Morley's buildings for Warwickshire County Cricket Club at Edgbaston. Along the M6 to the east of the city centre lies ShedKM's fantastic Fort Dunlop project for Urban Splash, and in Perry Beeches the city's own architects' department have produced a new school of real architectural quality. Despite the existence of these occasional highlights, there is still an urgent need for better-quality architecture and urban design throughout the city, but especially in the suburbs.

As Birmingham recovers from the damage inflicted in the 1960s and 70s, so the city has begun to regain some of its historic coherence. Streets that had been severed by several lanes of roaring traffic are slowly being reconnected, allowing people and vehicles to move more freely through the city's diverse neighbourhoods and quarters. The idea that Birmingham is a place in which people are happy to walk and explore is an unfamiliar but increasingly real phenomenon. Today, as well as throngs of office workers and shoppers there are also those who are there to simply look, amble and discover the city around them. The Birmingham that has been created over the past 20 years is not only a thriving commercial and cultural centre, but a city of reanimated streets and vibrant public spaces. The revitalised canals and the miles of pedestrian-friendly routes that criss-cross the city are an attraction in themselves. Today it is possible to walk, without ever encountering a car, from St Martin's Square in the south to Brindleyplace in the west – and new avenues for exploration are appearing all the time. Birmingham has come a long way from the concrete jungle created in the 1960s and 70s. The city has learnt some tough and difficult lessons and begun to slowly piece itself back together. Much has been achieved, and for those who know the city well the transformation has been remarkable. However, there remains much still to be done. No city, and least of all Birmingham, stands still for long and although far preferable to the recession and decline of the 1980s and early 1990s, economic growth brings its own pressures. Birmingham is now faced with another wave of redevelopment around the fringes of the old Inner Ring Road. The city's challenge will be to manage the social impact of this change, while continuing to strive for far higher standards in urban design and architecture.

NOTES

[1] By 1990, the NEC accounted for 42 per cent of the UK exhibition market.

[2] Sir Dick Knowles, Labour leader of Birmingham City Council from 1984 to 1993.

[3] Joe Holyoak, 'City Edge – before Brindleyplace', in *Brindleyplace: a model for urban regeneration*, edited by Ian Latham and Mark Swenarton, Right Angle Publishing Ltd, London, 1999, p. 21.

[4] The Birmingham Alliance is made up of Hammersons, Pearl Group Ltd and Land Securities.

[5] Fujifilm survey, quoted in http://news.bbc.co.uk/1/hi/england/west_midlands/4762807.stm, 11 May 2006.

[6] Chris Upton, *A History of Birmingham*, Phillimore, Chichester, 1993, p. 123.

[7] Adam Mornement, *No Longer Notorious, The Revival of Castle Vale, 1993–2005,* Castle Vale Housing Action Trust, Birmingham, 2005, p. 18.

[8] P. Jones & J. Evans, 'Urban regeneration, governance and the state: exploring notions of distance and proximity', *Urban Studies*, 2006, p. 7.

03
TRANSFORMING
THE SKYLINE

The projects in this chapter represent a diverse range
of typologies and design approaches. Some have been
included simply for the quality of their architecture, while
others demand attention due to the sheer scale of their
impact upon the city. Taken together, they demonstrate the
extent of the changes that have altered the landscape of
Birmingham so dramatically over the past two decades and
which will continue to shape the city into the future.

ARTS AND LEISURE

Birmingham's commitment to the arts today is a reflection of the city's long history as a cultural patron, and its current aspirations as a leading European city. Art and culture have been a focus for many cities seeking to reinvent themselves in recent years, but Birmingham can make a good claim to having pioneered this approach over many decades.

It was the first city in the country to provide municipal funding for its orchestra, dating back to the founding of the City of Birmingham Symphony Orchestra in 1920. Today the city provides vital financial support to a huge diversity of organisations, including the South Asian Arts group Sampad; the Drum, a centre for British Black and Asian art and culture; and ongoing support for the CBSO. High-quality buildings are essential to the ongoing success of Birmingham's artistic scene, and there have been particularly great strides made over the past 20 years towards improving the range and quality of the city's arts venues. Ever since the bold decision was made to build a new concert hall for the CBSO in the early 1980s, the city has marked itself out as being committed to a diverse and high-quality arts programme, underpinned by a huge investment in a series of stunning new buildings. Since that time, a whole series of new and renovated spaces have appeared across the city, including Stanton Williams's Gas Hall for the City Museum and Art Gallery and Associated Architects' new base for the Drum, in Handsworth. The examples illustrated here give just an indication of the extent of the transformation that the city's theatres, concert halls and galleries have undergone in the past few years.

The CBSO Centre is just one more example of Associated Architects' invaluable contribution to the city's built environment. It has provided the orchestra with a vital medium-sized rehearsal and performance space, allowing for a more experimental repertoire and for the CBSO to reach out to a more varied audience. The same practice's gloriously restored Hippodrome has also helped return that venerable Birmingham institution to its rightful place as a key destination for many of the country's best touring productions, as well as reinforcing its role as the home of the Birmingham Royal Ballet. The painstaking restoration is a complex but highly successful melding of the historic auditorium with stunning new foyers, rehearsal spaces and a vital new studio venue. Elsewhere in the city, Levitt Bernstein have provided the Ikon Gallery with a building that is commensurate with its international status. It has also given the gallery a profile within the city which it had never previously enjoyed.

Now, at the beginning of the 21st century, Birmingham's arts organisations and its most renowned artists and performers increasingly reflect the huge multicultural diversity of the city. The young Birmingham jazz saxophonist Soweto Kintch is a rising international star, while Birmingham has long been a recognised centre for the global bhangra music industry. With the emergence of a new generation of artists, the cultural diversity of the city is increasingly open and accessible to an ever-wider audience. Birmingham will, no doubt, continue its impressive commitment to the broadening of access and enjoyment of the arts, while the buildings presented here have already gone a huge way towards enriching the cultural horizons of the city.

CRAIG HOLMES/IMAGES OF BIRMINGHAM

The core of the project was to be a rehearsal hall capable of seating a full orchestra of 120 players together with the CBSO Chorus.

CITY OF BIRMINGHAM SYMPHONY ORCHESTRA CENTRE
ASSOCIATED ARCHITECTS

Berkley Street

Construction Value: £3.2 million
Completion Date: Spring 1998

Description
The centre provides a home for the CBSO, bringing all the orchestra's activities together in one building that includes a rehearsal hall. The centre is also a vibrant public performance space in use for chamber music, contemporary music and jazz.

History
Associated Architects was awarded the project in competition in 1992. Originally conceived as a conversion of an existing building, the introduction of the National Lottery and subsequent award of a grant enabled the CBSO to embark on a more ambitious new building on the same site. Ownership of its key facilities gives it independence, enhanced by an ability to generate income from public use of the rehearsal hall and foyer spaces.

Client's Brief
The core of the project was to be a rehearsal hall capable of seating a full orchestra of 120 players together with the CBSO Chorus. The acoustic had to be similar to that of Symphony Hall, with facilities to support recording and broadcast. Public use of the hall was critical to the business plan so a full range of ancillary space was required including a foyer with reception, bar and catering area. Offices for the Orchestra and the Birmingham Contemporary Music Group were to be provided and the building was to have a full range of support space including practice rooms, instrument storage, archive and library. In the transition of the project from conversion to new build the CBSO had become attached to the Berkley Street façade, which was to be retained in the completed scheme.

Design Process

A number of key design decisions informed the concept for the building. On a relatively restricted site there was an overriding logic to place the hall in the centre of the plan, surrounded by the other spaces to provide acoustic separation from the exterior. The hall itself had an optimum footprint and volume which defined its physical form, with a vaulted concrete roof. This was merged with the ancillary accommodation over three floors to cover the entire site footprint, corresponding with the retained façade to provide a building of similar height to its neighbours.

The orchestra was committed to a low energy solution, with excellent internal conditions for rehearsal: an unprecedented decision was taken to admit natural light into the hall at high level, with triple glazing to isolate noise break-in. Large volumes of fresh air are admitted using a displacement ventilation system, with extract at high level allowing for the natural buoyancy of the air. The system can be used for large periods of the year in a passive mode, with night purging at times of high external temperatures. The same concerns are extended to the other spaces in the building: exposed thermal mass in the form of concrete floors is employed and a multi-layer south-facing wall admits useful solar gain, controlled with natural ventilation and adjustable screening. The wall is designed as a steel grid infilled with glazing, buff brick and glass blocks.

The building budget was challenging, with principal elements including the hall having a high embedded cost. In this context a lean approach to construction was adopted using a restricted palate of building components delivered to the site and fixed in a completed state, without applied finishes. The internal aesthetic is directly derived from this approach: in the hall, timber for the floor, acoustic ceiling and technical balconies is set against coarse brick panels while adjustable acoustic drapes allow a range of acoustic attenuation. Brick and exposed concrete are the dominant materials in the ancillary spaces.

Several artists were commissioned to design and install works including the entrance doors, an inlaid carpet in the foyer, a glazed screen and metal sculpture in the bar.

Project Sign-off

The CBSO is an internationally acclaimed ambassador for Birmingham, and plays a significant role in the cultural life of the city. The centre is the first building of its type in the UK and provides a unique working environment for the orchestra, consolidating its position and providing an important small-scale venue for a wide range of music performance.

The project was reviewed in *The Architects' Journal* on 17 / 24 December 1998.

PROJECT TEAM

Client: **CBSO Society Ltd**
Architect: **Associated Architects**
Services Engineer: **Andrew Wilkes Management**
Structural Engineer: **Ove Arup & Partners**
Quantity Surveyor: **Faithful + Gould**
Acousticians: **ARTEC**

New 6,000 seat covered
spectator stand for the
international Test Cricket
Ground.

ERIC HOLLIES STAND

BRYANT PRIEST NEWMAN ARCHITECTS

Warwickshire County Cricket Club, Edgbaston Road

Construction Value: £2 million
Completion Date: April 2002

Description

New 6,000 seat covered spectator stand for the international Test Cricket Ground.

History

Following the successful completion of the Indoor Cricket Centre (see page 72), WCCC turned their attention to improving spectator facilities. The popular Eric Hollies Stand on the east of the ground was in a state of disrepair and was prioritised for improvements. The existing terracing was constructed of Second World War bomb rubble which had been tipped around the edge of the ground to help build the embankment in the 1940s / 50s. The site was awkward as it was squeezed between the boundary of the cricket field and the River Rea. Bryant Priest Newman Architects were appointed along with Price and Myers and Francis Graves to come up with proposals for a new stand.

Client's Brief

The brief for the project was to replace an existing terrace / embankment with a new stand increasing capacity by 1,300 and providing improved facilities and viewing for able bodied and disabled spectators. The design was developed using similar materials and principles used in other projects at Edgbaston by Bryant Priest Newman, to provide a consistent aesthetic. A particular visual link was created between the stand and the Indoor Cricket Centre designed in partnership with David Morley. These contrast sharply with rest of the development on the ground.

WCCC also required the redeveloped stand to be covered by a canopy and to be built for the budget of £2,100,000. It was also a requirement to include advertising boards on the roof. The entire construction work had to be carried out during the autumn, winter and early spring before the start of the cricket season and the first International Test Match.

Design Process

The concept for these elements was to provide simple flat, thin planes which conceal the simple structure above. Bryant Priest Newman wanted to create a series of roof planes that appear to hover above the crowd almost unsupported.

The articulation of the roofs into eight separate parasols (two per structural bay) allows the advertising boards, which were a requirement of WCCC, to be positioned away from the leading edge of each roof plane, expressing the thinness and allowing the effects of wind uplift to be dramatically reduced. The advertising boards are set in line with the roof ties and follow the same geometry, which signifies the split between front and rear roof.

The roofs are referred to as parasols or sun-shades as cricket is not played in the rain and spectators need to be shaded for the long periods of play during the summer days.

The four solid bays are linked together with lightweight stairs and louvres which indicate the change in geometry. This repetition is carried through to the underside of the stand where each bay is expressed and linked with the brick panels below. The lightweight cladding and the simple repetition ensured that the structural elements could be kept to a minimum by using standard sections in an innovative way, making the stand very economical. The brick panels described above are red and stack bonded to link with the terracotta wall of the Indoor Cricket Centre.

Whilst The England and Wales Cricket Board advise Cricket Clubs / grounds to budget for around £1,000 per seat for new stands, The Eric Hollies Stand equates to around £650 per seat.

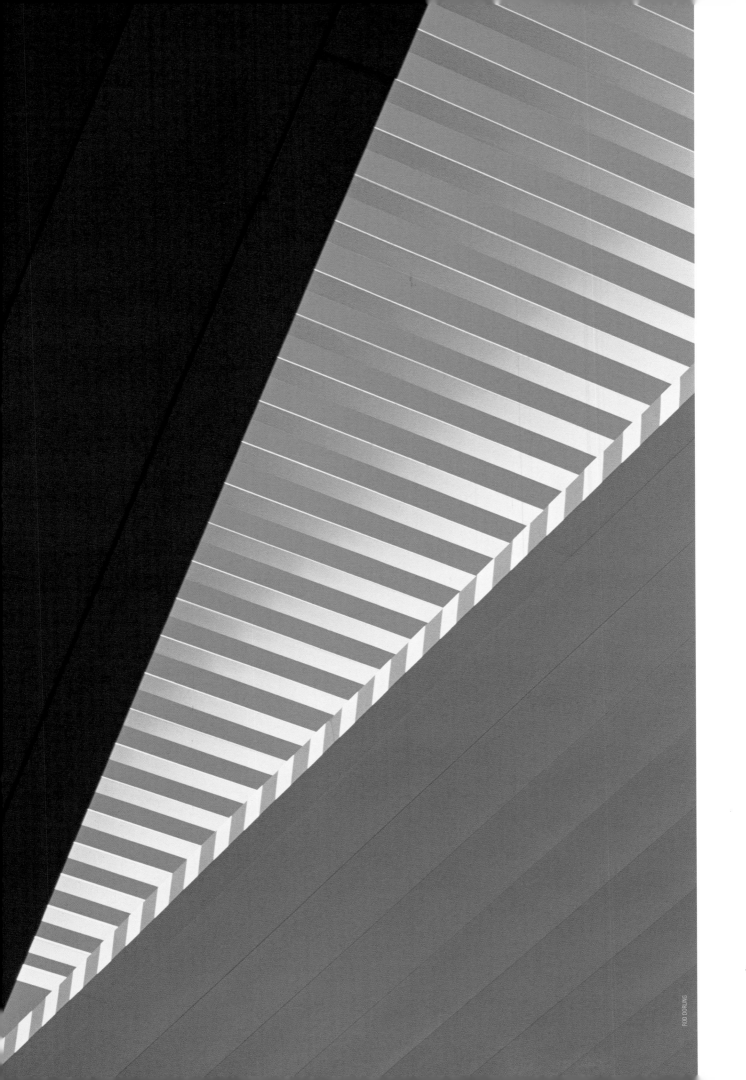

49

ROD DORLING

ROD DORLING

Project Sign-off

The stand has received many awards and commendations since its completion. These include winning the award for best use of aluminium in a building by a young practice in the 2003 Imagination Awards, a certificate of merit in the 2003 Structural Steel Design awards and winner of the Leisure and Recreation category of the local authority Built in Quality Awards 2002. The project reached the shortlist of five schemes for the region in the 2003 RIBA Awards and was also short-listed in the 2003 British Construction Industry awards.

The Architects' Journal and *Building Magazine* have featured the stand with *Building Magazine* saying the following:

'Bryant Priest Newman manages to combine simplicity and elegance with a remarkably low cost.'

Building Magazine 25 October 2002

PROJECT TEAM

Client: **Warwickshire County Cricket Club**
Architect: **Bryant Priest Newman Architects**
Structural Engineer: **Price & Myers**
Quantity Surveyor: **Francis Graves**

ROD DORLING

51

The principal objective of the brief was to strengthen and extend the Hippodrome's position through enhanced provision for its audiences, actors, dancers, musicians and staff.

BIRMINGHAM HIPPODROME
ASSOCIATED ARCHITECTS LLP AND LDN ARCHITECTS

Birmingham Hippodrome Theatre, Hurst St, Birmingham B5 4BT

Construction Value: £24 million
Completion Date: October 2001

Description

The Birmingham Hippodrome is Britain's leading independent theatre and the home of Birmingham Royal Ballet and DanceXchange. The rebuilding, extension and refurbishment of the theatre has provided Birmingham with a first class performing arts amenity.

The building won an RIBA Regional Award in 2003.

History

The origins of the Hippodrome Theatre date back to 1899 but the current auditorium dates from 1924 and is the work of Burdwood and Mitchell Architects of London. In enlarging the capacity of the theatre they constructed a single massive circle which extended through the rear wall of the original theatre and into the upper part of the older Assembly Rooms. This was to form one of the structural challenges of this project as the auditorium was to be retained and the Assembly Rooms building – then the front of house facilities – was to be demolished. In 1985 the stage and fly tower were greatly increased and the Birmingham Royal Ballet arrived in 1990 in an adjacent building. This firmly established the Birmingham Hippodrome as a leading receiving house for lyric theatre.

Client's Brief

The principal objective of the brief was to strengthen and extend the Hippodrome's position through enhanced provision for its audiences, actors, dancers, musicians and staff.

The theatre's key assets were the stage and fly tower and the distinguished but unlisted Edwardian auditorium. The remainder of the theatre was in a poor and generally inadequate condition to meet the needs of the 21st century. One hundred years of improvisation around existing structures had produced a mean entrance foyer, narrow corridors, cramped and windowless bars and restaurants and inadequate facilities for the elderly and disabled.

The theatre trust had the foresight to acquire two large adjacent sites and started to form a vision for a new complex that would transform the activities and facilities of the theatre. Following a competition they forged an unusual collaboration of two architectural practices for the project and jointly appointed Associated Architects of Birmingham and LDN Architects from Edinburgh. A detailed brief was developed and a successful bid for substantial Arts Lottery funding was made. The redevelopment, which marked the theatre's centenary, was also seen as a catalyst for the regeneration of the wider theatre district and Chinese quarter on the southern fringes of the city centre. The detail brief builds on the 1,900 seat auditorium and stage house and includes a new 200 seat studio theatre, large dance studios, new front of house facilities and a centre for the treatment and research of dance injuries, a new get in and rear stage area. The clients also required the new building to be a model of excellence in accessibility and integration of public art.

Design Process

A clear understanding of what already existed formed the springboard for the design concept. Our analysis revolved around three issues – the strengths and weaknesses of the site; the historic value and potential of the existing spaces; and the adjacent land acquisitions – and their potential to respond to the 21st-century requirements of the Hippodrome. The retention and enhancement of the features of the Edwardian auditorium were conceptually and literally central to the design. The strategic response to the brief was to distil a wide range of aims and ambitions set by the Hippodrome into a solution that achieves for all the building's users a sense of cohesiveness, clarity, accessibility, practicality and delight.

The new development involved the refurbishment of the Edwardian auditorium, demolition and rebuilding of the front of house, foyers, restaurant and bars, and the improvement of rear stage facilities. Additionally a seven-storey extension was inserted linking the BRB building with the auditorium and foyers. The new extension provides accommodation for the 200-seat Patrick Centre for the Performing Arts; dressing rooms; hospitality suites; theatre administration offices and large dance studios for BRB and DanceXchange; a new Green Room; Administration Offices and the Jerwood Centre for the Prevention and Treatment of Dance Injuries that includes a hydrotherapy pool with underwater cameras.

The project divides into four distinctive elements: Front of House; Auditorium; Back of House; and a major new building to the north. Within the Auditorium, a mid-circle entrance was inserted by flying the building over the footpath below. Seating was completely replaced to include appropriate seating for a range of disabilities in both tiers, a fire curtain artwork canvas added, and the auditorium redecorated in a rich crimson, purple, plum, cream and silver leaf colour scheme. Glass chandeliers from the original front of house have been re-located in the side boxes of the auditorium. The previous front of house was demolished, and the Hippodrome given a street presence with projecting prow to announce the building to the city centre. The change in level at the entrance is made by steps and a wide ramp both given equal importance. The foyer tapers from the entrance to accentuate the visual drama of the journey past the box office and retail spaces to the full height atrium housing the bars, stairs and lifts. The theatrical experience is further enhanced for patrons as they move through generous stairs and bridges or look across the deep voids of the main foyer.

The internal areas were rationalised and levels were co-ordinated, and natural light was brought into the centre of the building with full height glazed elements onto Hurst Street to the north east, Inge Street to the south east and Thorp Street to the north west.

The project involved commissioning a Public Art Consultant and collaboration with artists for major pieces of public art. Balraj Khanna was commissioned after a competition for a fire curtain design. Some of the colours of the latter were picked out and formed the palette for the interior decoration of the whole complex. The curtain was painted in-situ. Liz Rideal was responsible for the engraving on the fully glazed elevation to the grand staircase. Her curtain swag theme was felt to be particularly appropriate for a theatre and is further developed in the lantern that hangs through the central staircase well.

Externally the new building creates a sense of place with the drama of the building taken onto the streets through the various large glazed elements. The entrance now engages with the pedestrianised Hurst Street, and at night the entrance foyer spaces are clearly on display, while patrons enjoy views across the city from the restaurant and hospitality spaces. The stage door and new wing fronting Thorp Street have a strong identity and street presence, which is a deliberate contrast to the post-modern façade of the adjacent BRB building. A subtle blend of contrasting materials has been used which includes a planar glass front wall between dark green slate piers and a projecting silver canopy and prow. The corner is turned in terracotta tiles which join to the brick and terracotta elevation of the 1899 auditorium. The new circle access is expressed in projecting floating copper panels.

The new wing to the north is a simpler essay in white render, grey metal windows and suspended planar glass atrium wall exposing a dramatic metal staircase and blue wall signalling the circulation zone at each level. This intervention off Thorp Street incorporates a variety of functions and activities. A striking dance studio for BRB and generous studios for DanceXchange, together with a new performing arts theatre with an independent Thorp Street entrance are among many additions. Acoustic isolation of the spaces required particular structural solutions and the brief requirement for 'openness' has resulted in a carefully crafted top lit atrium that also gives the additional benefit of energy conservation, including bringing natural light and ventilation to the dressing rooms in the basement.

Lottery funding, EU grants, Birmingham City funding and public and corporate sponsorship paid for the project. Architects were appointed in 1996; work began on site in April 1999 and was completed in October 2001.

Project Sign-off

CABE's Case Study Evaluation of the project summarises The Birmingham Hippodrome project as being a huge exercise in rationalising and meshing together of what existed into a coherent whole with skilful interventions and additions, adding up to more than the sum of its parts.

The project was published and reviewed in *The Architects Journal* on 14 March 2002.

PROJECT TEAM

Client: **The Birmingham Hippodrome Theatre Trust**
Architect: **Associated Architects LLP and LDN Architects**
Project Manager: **Elias Topping**
Quantity Surveyor: **EC Harris**
Structural Engineers: **Buro Happold**
Services Engineer: **Buro Happold**
Acousticians: **Sandy Brown Associates**
Planning Supervisors : **Associated Architects**
Access Consultants: **Earnscliffe Davies Associates**
Public Arts Consultant: **PACA**
Catering Design: **Intracat Limited**
Main Contractor: **HBG Construction Limited**

In the mid 1980s an application for EU funding was successful and over the next 6 years planning procurement and realisation took place, ending in the opening by Queen Elizabeth in 1991.

INTERNATIONAL CONVENTION CENTRE

CAPITA PERCY THOMAS

Broad Street, Birmingham

Construction Value: £136 million
Completion Date: February 1992

Description

The International Convention Centre is a vast complex of conference halls and executive rooms grouped around a landscaped mall extending the full height and length of the building. The facility played a crucial role during the 1990s in changing perceptions of the city and stimulating further investment. The huge complex forms a key link in the pedestrian route that connects Centenary Square and the rest of the city centre to the burgeoning canal-side developments, typified by Brindleyplace and the Mailbox.

History

The City of Birmingham decided in the early 1980s that a major initiative was needed to help reposition the city's economy and image to address the increasingly service-led British economy. The decision was made to construct a city-centre convention facility that would complement the NEC and build upon its global success. The project also provided the opportunity to realise the long-held dream of a new world-class concert hall for the City of Birmingham Symphony Orchestra and its young and ambitious conductor, Simon Rattle.

The council were also keenly aware of the potential the project offered for regenerating the once-prosperous Broad Street area. The site, formerly a brewery and ageing Victorian-era exhibition hall, was a major un-used land resource in a key strategic location. It had previously been ear-marked for redevelopment as part of a gigantic and never completed civic centre scheme in the 1930s and lay along a key east–west route into the city centre.

In the mid-1980s an application for EU funding was successful and over the next 6 years planning procurement and realisation took place, ending in the opening by Queen Elizabeth in 1991.

The inaugural event was to stage the Olympic Committee selection process in 1991 which attracted the world's media to the venue and was a PR coup.

Client's Brief

Birmingham City Council decided that the central driver for regeneration of the city would be a major conference centre venue that would capitalise on the logistic benefits of the city's central UK location. The components of the brief were to capitalise on the heritage aspects of the area and to retain key site features.

The key elements of the ICC brief were:

Hall 1 – 1,500 seat conference format with seats housing fold away tables and lamps

Hall 2 – 2,200 seat acoustically excellent Concert Hall for delegates and visitors

Hall 3 – flat floor hall of 3,000 m^2 – accommodating 2,000 diners and 2,900 delegates

Hall 4 – 800 m^2 for 600 diners or 800 delegates

Hall 5 – auditorium seating 300 with convertible desks and translation booths

Halls 6 to 11 – sub-divisible meeting rooms seating 30 to 300 in contained suites

The complex was to become the crossroads of new key routes through the city via canal bridges, the Brindleyplace development, the National Indoor Arena and Centenary Square.

The design was to reduce the impact of the 1960s strategy to separate cars and people and return the pedestrian to dominance within the city. The City Council had a further ambition to make the complex attractive to the citizens of Birmingham as well as to international conference delegates.

The concert hall, the most technically challenging element of the project, was to be located directly above the mainline railway leading from Birmingham to Manchester.

Design Process

The convention market was relatively young to the UK at the inception of the project. Consequently, it was decided to do three things:

> research the world's best facilities
> employ a market leader in conference venue briefing
> select a design and construction team with flair and experience in the sector.

The NEC initiative to harness the central UK location for major exhibitions was strategically and commercially very successful. In view of this and the long gestation period of the project a virtual team was selected as 'Clients' to the design team. The NEC virtual team worked with the design team to ensure that operational experience from the NEC complex on commercial, catering, facility management and complex operational issues would be fed into the design process well before the final management team were appointed.

The design team numbered over 200 personnel and consequently communication was given a high priority.

Amongst the consultants employed on the project were New York-based Artec, experts in acoustics and concert venues. Artec's involvement in the project led to the highly sophisticated acoustic solutions that characterise Symphony Hall and have contributed to it being widely regarded as one of the world's finest classical music venues. Amongst the numerous innovative features is the use of hundreds of rubber pads to isolate the hall from the railway that runs underneath.

The centre is divided into two halves by the dramatic mall that links Centenary Square to the canal-side and Brindleyplace. Symphony Hall lies to the south of the mall, with most of the convention halls located to the north. The building addresses Centenary Square through a huge glass entrance canopy and massive faceted window that fronts the Symphony Hall foyers. At its rear, the building steps down to address the more intimate scale of the canal.

Project Sign-off

Since its opening the Convention Centre has played host to a string of high-profile gatherings, including the first full gathering of the G8 in 1998. As intended, the ICC has played a key role in changing international perceptions of the city and helped attract significant new investment to a previously run-down area of the city. As a home for the CBSO, Symphony Hall has proved to be a huge success and an immense source of pride for the people of Birmingam.

MARKETING BIRMINGHAM

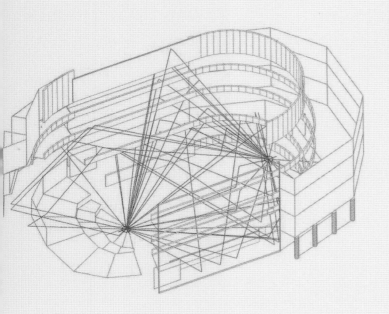

PROJECT TEAM

Client: **Birmingham City Council**

Lead Architects: **Capita Percy Thomas**

Theatre Consultants: **RHWL**

Structural and Mechanical / Electrical Engineering: **Ove Arup & Partners**

Project Management: **Bucknall Austin**

Quantity Surveyors: **Silk & Frazier**

Acousticians: **Artec – New York**

Interior Design: **CPT**

Landscape Design: **CPT**

Conference Dynamics: **Spectrum Communications**

Main Contractor: **Turner-Douglas (Interserve)**

The original school, designed in a robust and decorative Ruskinian Gothic style, was extended by the same architects in the 1890s and further extensions were built around 1910.

IKON GALLERY
LEVITT BERNSTEIN

1 Oozells Square, Brindleyplace, Birmingham B1 2HS

Construction Value: £3.85 million
Completion Date: December 1997

Description
The conversion of a derelict Victorian Board School to create an art gallery to display temporary exhibitions by living artists.

History
In late 1991 Ikon Gallery started looking for a new home because the lease on their existing premises was coming to an end. Of all the options considered, and despite its totally ruinous state, Oozells Street School had the greatest potential.

It was built in 1877 to the design of Martin & Chamberlain, Birmingham's premier Victorian architects, who built over 40 board schools – of which but a handful survive – as well as the Art School (see page 76). The original school, designed in a robust and decorative Ruskinian Gothic style, was extended by the same architects in the 1890s and further extensions were built around 1910. A tower was a feature of all their schools and was used as part of the natural ventilation system. At Oozells Street the tower was removed for safety in the 1960s.

After Brindleyplace changed hands in 1994, the conversion of the school into an art gallery became an intrinsic part of the developer's plans for the area. While the plans were being developed and lottery money secured, Brindleyplace Plc demolished all the 20th-century extensions in 1995 and, under the direction of Levitt Bernstein Associates, undertook an external repairs contract to arrest the deterioration.

Client's Brief
Ikon Gallery was already well established in John Bright Street when it started to look for a larger, more permanent base for its temporary and touring exhibitions. In addition to gallery space, it required a

café, bookshop, education space, resource area, offices, workshop, storage, plant and ancillary accommodation. The brief called for the architects to provide the following:

> a building for the people of Birmingham that they would feel comfortable entering (unlike the old premises which were intimidating);

> an experience for the gallery visitor that was enjoyable and exciting;

> encouragement for visitors to move up through the building into the gallery spaces;

> gallery spaces that were welcoming to visitors yet versatile enough to accommodate the range of contemporary art;

> spaces which artists could respond to and where it was possible to change walls, surfaces etc. (i.e. not a 'museum' environment);

> good access to the exhibition floors for all shapes and sizes of works of art.

Design Process
The Layout

The Ikon Gallery is devoted to showing temporary exhibitions of the works of living artists, with much emphasis on education, interpretation and attracting new visitors to contemporary art.

The school building is H-shaped in plan and three storeys high. The large, linked classrooms on the first and second floors are converted to provide 450 m² of gallery space. The ground floor contains the entrance, a shop, a café and support spaces for both the public and the works of art. A new basement is dug out to provide further storage, workshop and plant areas.

As a school the building had no main entrance, simply doors onto two stairs, one for boys and the other for girls and infants. These two stairs become escape routes, and a new entrance is created in the front elevation. In order to keep the uninterrupted sequence of exhibition spaces, new stairs and lifts for the public and for servicing are added outside the original building in a simple elegant modern fashion, contrasting with the highly detailed red brick.

The route to the galleries, via a glass stair in a glazed enclosure, is intended to be an exhilarating process,

both a point of reference for visitors and a prelude for pedestrians approaching from Centenary Square. Late receipt of a European grant enabled the tower to be rebuilt and, as originally, it forms part of the ventilation design; internally its full height is a feature of the process of entering the building, which can be enjoyed on all three levels.

The Galleries

An important principle of the design is to ensure that the route around the building is exciting and visually interesting, without impinging upon the concentrated enjoyment of the exhibits within the gallery spaces. There is, therefore, a change of pace within the galleries themselves, which are restrained and simple conversions of the original rooms; the first floor is air conditioned to conservation standard and has tall flat-ceilinged rooms with the option of side light. The top floor has lofty spaces with a variety of exposed trusses and the option of top and side lighting.

As a much-admired existing building it was already accepted as an attractive environment, and the many changes it has undergone suggested an ability to adapt to the variety of ways in which artists and curators may wish to use it. It was very much felt that the intrinsic character of the old school, combined with its malleability as a well-worn building, would inspire artists either to adapt or work with it to show their works in the most interesting way.

The galleries need to respond to artists working in different scales and in a variety of media. They need, on different occasions, to be museum, showroom or studio, demanding a level of neutrality. A visibly flexible space has not been called for, however, because the artists in their turn may wish to interact with the building. The quality of the spaces is intended to engender a positive dialogue between the building and the art, and be a comfortable and welcoming environment for frequent and new visitors alike.

The External Environment

The surrounding developments had altered the adjoining ground levels, and a virtue has been made of this fact by setting the building on a dark slate plinth. This proposal was one of the results of the collaboration with the artist Tania Kovats, following receipt of an Art for Architecture

award from the Royal Society of Arts. Following the creation of the plinth, which expresses itself as a threshold for the entrance and terrace for the café, the Brindleyplace masterplan was adapted to respond with the creation of Oozells Square.

Project Sign-off

The gallery opened in March 1998. From the perspective of providing an enjoyable and interesting environment for people to come and see contemporary art, it has been an overwhelming success. To quote one of the front of house staff: 'Even if they don't like the art, at least the building makes them happy!'

As a contemporary art gallery, the needs of artists are paramount. Ikon has shown the full range of installation, sculpture, painting, video and film. Exhibiting artists have been very complimentary about the spaces, as have artists who have visited.

PROJECT TEAM

Client: **Ikon Gallery**
Architect: **Levitt Bernstein**
Quantity Surveyor: **Silk and Frazier**
Structural Engineer: **Peel and Fowler**
Services Engineer: **H.L. Dawson and Partners**
Lighting: **John Johnson: Lightwaves**
Graphic Designer: **Rose-Innes Associates**
Artist: **Tania Kovats**
Catering Consultant: **Cadbury Ltd**
Acoustic Consultant: **Noise Advisory Services**
Main Contractor: **Carillion Plc**

COMMUNITY AND LEARNING

The foundations of successful communities often lie in the network of institutions and educational establishments that help stitch together different individuals, families and diverse cultural groups. These institutions, from self-help groups to higher-education establishments, have often had to make do with inadequate and dilapidated buildings, and much of their work has been achieved despite their surroundings rather than because of them.

For many years during the 1970s and 80s, the public infrastructure of Britain seemed to be in a perilous decline towards neglect and outright collapse, and Birmingham was no different to any other UK city in this respect. A number of changes during the late 1980s and 90s began to turn this situation around, not least of which was the advent of the National Lottery in 1995. Where there had previously only been cash-strapped councils and under-funded government departments, the National Lottery paved the way for an unprecedented period of building right the way across Birmingham. Several of the projects in this book are the result of Lottery funding, and this chapter in particular is a testament to the tremendous transformation that it precipitated throughout the country.

The projects collected together here give some sense of the wealth of buildings that has emerged across Birmingham in recent years with the purpose of fostering learning and community activity.

Amongst the very best new small buildings to have appeared in the city over the past decade is Blakesley Hall Visitor Centre in Yardley by Niall Phillips Architects. This Bristol-based practice has brought a highly sympathetic and yet strongly contemporary architectural approach to the complex and difficult job of building in the context of an historic structure. Blakesley Hall itself was

a much-loved but under-utilised local museum when Niall Phillips was handed the job of restoring the old house and adding a new visitor centre and community facilities. It is one of a handful of medieval structures still standing within Birmingham, and is therefore a highly treasured part of the city's urban fabric and history. The new buildings, restoration work and historical garden are a model of how to add sensitively but creatively to older buildings. It must be hoped that Blakesley Hall points the way to a successful future for Birmingham's other historic houses and museums.

Elsewhere in this chapter, projects such as David Morley's and Bryant Priest Newman's Indoor Cricket Centre at Edgbaston and Millennium Point in Eastside demonstrate a far more uncompromisingly modern approach that has given the city a much-needed architectural boost. The Indoor Cricket Centre in particular, which followed on from a similar project by David Morley at Lords, has shown that good architecture and excellent sporting facilities can go hand in hand. Too often in Birmingham, stadiums and recreational facilities have been treated as architectural afterthoughts. Morley and BPN have demonstrated that the highest quality design can be achieved on an extremely tight budget and without apparent compromise.

At the forefront of grassroots community development in Birmingham are institutions like the Afro-Caribbean Millennium Centre, which promotes learning and skills in the deprived Winson Green area of the city. The building, by Birmingham-based D5 Architects, is a literal and metaphorical symbol of the ongoing importance of the contribution that the Afro-Caribbean community has made to the city. Built on a prominent site on the Dudley Road, the centre offers exciting opportunities to many young people who might otherwise be left feeling unchallenged by an education system that too often seems to allow youngsters to slip through the net. Like many of the best buildings in *Shaping the City*, it is a reminder of just what can be achieved when the people of Birmingham work imaginatively together to realise their collective potential.

AFRO-CARIBBEAN MILLENNIUM CENTRE (ACMC)
D5 ARCHITECTS LLP

329–339 Dudley Road, Winson Green, Birmingham

Construction Value: £1.2 million
Completion Date: March 2004

Description

A new-build structure designed to accommodate various community facilities, including a locally broadcast radio station.

History

The building is located in Winson Green, one of the most socially deprived areas in the country and a designated urban regeneration zone. The centre stands on the former site of a Victorian terrace, two units of which had been occupied by the ACMC.

Client's Brief

'This project will increase opportunities, diversify the arts, promote innovation, creativity and excellence, invest in new talent and increase resources for the arts in an area suffering from high levels of social exclusion. Consequently it will empower the community and change people's lives.'

The ACMC is a progressive organisation with a high-profile local and international reputation. The completed building was required to further promote awareness of the centre to the local community and act as a catalyst for regeneration within the area. The centre had to provide services including social welfare, employment resources, senior citizens' activities and programmes for young people, through a range of facilities including business-incubation units, multimedia suites, a radio station, a recording studio and various general-purpose rooms.

Design Process

Whilst the new building is expressly modern, the façade was composed with a historical rhythm of four sections over two stories with a unifying third storey across the top. Each section is organised with solid or void elements formed from glazing and insulated render panels, whose composition is individual to each bay. To contrast with the render-and-glass composition, the entrance bay employs oak cladding to the first floor and entrance door below. This creates a vertical axis which works in collaboration with a feature canopy, clearly expressing the main entrance when viewed against the predominantly horizontal nature of the façade.

The building has as many passive environmental controls as possible. Fixed louvres are positioned over the first-floor windows and horizontal *brise-soleil* provide protection to the shallower second-floor windows. The use of three forms of solar protection acts to provide articulation and interest to the façade whilst also communicating the different uses within each floor upon the elevation.

Internally, the building has been designed to be light and airy, with a simple and honest approach to materials. All steelwork is exposed and painted grey to match the external treatment. The ceilings are the same structural concrete planks used to form the floors, which provide thermal mass to passively modulate heat gain in the summer months. Much of the electrical and mechanical installation is designed to be exposed and expressed, rather than hidden – a feature particularly evident in the radio-station corridor where mechanical services are up-lit.

Project Sign-off

The first phase of development demanded significant time and energy from the design team, and in particular the client, to obtain the necessary funding. However, dedication by the client organisation in committing to the ethos of the centre's purpose helped exceed expectations and the design team were instructed to commence design work for the extension upon completion of the first phase. The building and the services it contains are proving themselves to have met and exceeded the brief to engage the whole community with a positive focus for local regeneration.

PROJECT TEAM

Client: **Afro-Caribbean Millennium Centre Limited**
Architect: **D5 Architects LLP**
Main Contractor: **Weaver Plc**
Quantity Surveyor: **Allsebrook & Hadley**
Structural Engineer: **Ove Arup & Partners**
Services Engineer: **Ove Arup & Partners**
Project Manager: **Phoenix Beard**
Planning Supervisor: **D5 Architects LLP**
Party Wall Surveyor: **Phoenix Beard**
Radio Studio Design and Construction: **Oxford Sound & Media**
Project Facilitator: **Tony Collier Associates**

The University of Birmingham wanted a facility that would bring together a number of the largest NMR spectrometers in the world.

THE HENRY WELLCOME BUILDING FOR BIOMOLECULAR NMR SPECTROSCOPY

BERMAN GUEDES STRETTON

University of Birmingham, Edgbaston, Birmingham

Construction Value: £2.58 million
Completion Date: August 2005

Description

The Henry Wellcome Building for Biomolecular NMR Spectroscopy at the University of Birmingham is a state-of-the-art national facility for biological molecular research.

History

Commissioned by the University in collaboration with the Wellcome Trust in 2002, the 980 m² building is situated on a sloping greenfield site which forms part of the University's Edgbaston Campus. Early analysis of vibration and radio-frequency interference sources determined the specific site in an exclusion zone some 150 m from the passing railway.

Client's Brief

Nuclear Magnetic Resonance or 'NMR' spectroscopy is a rapidly growing area of scientific interest, which uses extreme magnetic fields in the study of the nuclei of cell structures. The University of Birmingham wanted a facility that would bring together a number of the largest NMR spectrometers in the world.

Design Process

For the design team, one of the most challenging aspects of the scheme was how to resolve the complex technical issues associated with the highly sensitive NMR equipment. Chief amongst these was how to maintain a precise temperature of between plus and minus 0.5°C in the three spectroscopy chambers. In addition, the structure and fabric of the chambers needed to minimise any form of vibration, use only non-ferrous construction and be capable of clear-spanning 13 m (the diameter of the largest spectrometer's magnetic field). To this end, it was decided to exploit the building's thermal mass in the form of dense, load-bearing masonry walls supporting in-situ concrete roofs.

At the heart of the plan are three separate NMR chambers: two housing single high-powered spectrometers and one combining three smaller spectrometers. These are expressed as independent masonry-clad pavilions separated by 'glass-slot' rooflights. Magnetic fields or gauss radials determine the footprint of each chamber. This ensures that the magnetic fields, which could be harmful to passers-by fitted with pacemakers, are fully contained by the enclosing walls – but also, conversely, that passers-by do not affect readings from the instruments.

A single computer console area for NMR operators is positioned to allow a visual link between activities within each chamber via full-height glazed screens. The aperture for these screens is sized to allow the spectrometer's installation, and the screens are demountable for future flexibility. The building entrance hall is arranged to allow maximum flexibility in use, with an open area for seminars and presentations. Offices and ancillary functions are contained in a free-standing timber clad 'box', whose upper deck provides an open 'breakout' space overlooking the entrance hall. Plant occupies the upper floor continuously along the rear of the building, abutting each chamber to allow mechanical ventilation. A laboratory and other ancillary accommodation occupy the space beneath.

The chambers themselves are mechanically ventilated with 95 per cent of the air recirculated to minimise the need for preheating. The entrance foyer is naturally ventilated to offset the energy consumption of the chambers. Solar gain is minimised in the entrance space by an oversailing roof and external timber louvres fixed to the curtain wall of the seminar space. Rooflights allow natural light into deep-plan spaces. These are orientated to prevent solar gain. Rooflights in the entrance area are openable via actuators controlled by a BMS system as part of the natural ventilation strategy.

Natural self-finished materials are used throughout. Avoiding the use of suspended ceilings and plasterboard finishes, funds were instead diverted to providing high-quality concrete and timber surfaces.

Project Sign-off

The NMR facility is the culmination of a highly collaborative effort to create a beautiful and legible building within the constraints of a very exacting set of requirements. There are few precedents for this building type, a fact which allowed the freedom to bring something more to the scheme than a direct response to the brief. The interest it is continuing to generate is an accomplishment for all those who have contributed to its realisation.

PROJECT TEAM

Client: **University of Birmingham**
Architect: **Berman Guedes Stretton**
Main Contractor: **Morrison Construction**
Quantity Surveyor: **Robinson Low Francis**
Structural Engineer: **Scott Wilson Peel and Fowler**
Services Engineer: **Stewart Associates**
Planning Supervisor: **RLF H&S**
Lighting Consultant: **LAPD**

The building has been designed so that it is closely integrated into the landscaping and becomes part of the experience of the gardens.

BLAKESLEY HALL
NIALL PHILLIPS ARCHITECTS LTD

Blakesley Hall, Yardley Birmingham

Construction Value: £2.5 million
Completion Date: March 2002

Description

The repair and conservation of a Grade II* 16th- and 17th-century timber-framed hall, currently used as a museum by the City of Birmingham; the construction of a new visitor building with new car parking and road access provision; and the extension of the landscaped gardens.

History

Blakesley Hall is a Grade II* listed timber-framed Elizabethan yeoman's house constructed in 1590. The Hall is owned by Birmingham City Council and has been used as a museum since the 1970s.

The contract value of the project was £2.5 million. Works began on site in March 2001 and the buildings were opened again to the public in May 2002.

Client's Brief

The architects were commissioned in 1998 to develop a scheme for the Hall and site that would help provide it with a secure, sustainable future. This was to be done by improving its potential as an important regional visitor attraction and a viable facility for schools, visitors and the community. The brief encompassed alterations and conservation works to the Hall, alongside the provision both of improved educational facilities within the 17th-century listed brick barn and of new visitor facilities. The whole site was landscaped to improve the setting and security of the Hall and to provide a new vehicular entrance and additional on-site car parking.

Design Process

A key part of the site strategy was to extend the site to the north of the Hall by utilising a redundant bowling green. This enabled the gardens to be significantly expanded and re-landscaped, thereby greatly improving the setting of the Hall and providing additional space for car and coach

parking to the rear. The visitor building is located in the north west corner of the gardens, where it forms the new entry point to the grounds, has minimal impact on the Hall and enables visitors to approach the Hall through the attractive setting of the gardens.

The new building is deliberately reticent in its scale and choice of materials in order not to dominate the relatively small scale of the Hall, and is divided into two single-storey wings to further lessen its visual impact on the site. The building has been designed so that it is closely integrated into the landscaping and becomes part of the experience of the gardens. The use of garden walls and hedges extending from the building provides a formal enclosure to the grounds, roots the building within the landscaping, and provides physical security to the Hall. The garden paths are continued below the timber pergola to form the circulation within the building, with external materials and detailing used internally to increase the perception of circulating within the garden setting.

The new visitor centre is constructed using materials that will weather naturally and complement the existing buildings, but it is carefully detailed in a contemporary manner so as not to confuse the new and historic buildings. It is constructed of load-bearing masonry, using traditional soft lime mortars to avoid movement joints. The pitched roofs over each wing are supported on exposed steel trusses and are clad in handmade plain tiles. The glazed pergola to the garden is in unfinished Western Red Cedar, with terne-coated stainless-steel roofing which will weather to a lead grey.

The Hall underwent an extensive programme of repair and alteration works, and was re-serviced with discreet lighting and modern detection and alarm systems. Internally, many obtrusive fittings, including toilets and a large boiler room,

were removed to the new building to allow a number of the spaces to be reinstated as period rooms. The Hall was completely redecorated internally and externally to recreate more accurately the colours and finishes that would have been used in the 16th century. The 17th-century brick barn was adapted to form two large spaces for visiting groups of schoolchildren and for community activities, with a central service core carefully detailed to contrast with the existing historic fabric.

The grounds and gardens were extensively landscaped with new herb beds and planting themes that draw historical reference from the Hall and the local area.

Project Sign-off

The scheme has revitalised a much-loved local resource within the Yardley area, and helped raise the museum's profile within the city. The project is an exemplary instance of a single architectural practice working at once on both historical conservation and sensitive contemporary new-build. The resulting complex of new visitor centre, imaginative landscaping and beautifully restored historic house is one of the most successful architectural compositions in Birmingham of the past decade.

ALL IMAGES ON THIS SPREAD CRAIG HOLMES/IMAGES OF BIRMINGHAM

PROJECT TEAM

Client: **Birmingham City Council: Museums and Art Gallery**

Architect: **Niall Phillips Architects Ltd**

Main Contractor: **William Sapcote and Sons Ltd**

Quantity Surveyor: **Urban Design Department, Birmingham City Council**

Structural Engineer (Barn and New Visitor Building): **Urban Design Department, BCC**

Services Engineer: **Urban Design Department, BCC**

Landscape Architect: **Eden Design**

General Archaeologist: **Urban Design Department, BCC**

As a result of the brief, the design team created a naturally lit and naturally ventilated facility, thus ensuring that the building is highly cost and energy efficient.

EDGBASTON INDOOR CRICKET CENTRE
BRYANT PRIEST NEWMAN ARCHITECTS JOINTLY WITH DAVID MORLEY ARCHITECTS

Warwickshire County Cricket Club, Edgbaston Road, Birmingham

Construction Value: £2.4 million
Completion Date: March 2000

Description

Modern, low-energy, naturally lit and naturally ventilated purpose-built eight-lane indoor cricket centre with ancillary accommodation, including changing rooms, offices, shop, bar and audio-visual room.

History

In accordance with Sports Lottery rules, Warwickshire County Cricket Club interviewed several architects to design an Indoor Cricket Centre of Excellence at Edgbaston. Following a split decision, the committee approached David Morley Architects of London and Bryant Priest Newman Architects of Birmingham to work together to design a state-of-the-art purpose-built eight-lane cricket centre to be a landmark building for the club and the city.

David Morley Architects had won several RIBA and other awards, and have worked extensively at Lords Cricket Ground. Bryant Priest Newman Architects were the only Midlands architects to be included in *New Architects: A Guide to Britain's Best Young Architectural Practices*, published by the Architecture Foundation in association with the Department for Culture, Media and Sport in 1998.

Client's Brief

The client's budget was £2.4m, with £1.65m coming from the Sports Lottery Fund. This equates to a rate of £875 per square metre, which is remarkably cheap for an RIBA award-winning building. This figure also includes the surrounding landscaping. As with all Lottery projects, capital funds are provided but not revenue funding. It was crucial to the client that the design team create a low-energy, low-maintenance design to ensure exceptionally low running costs. Again, common to all Lottery-funded projects is the requirement to create a fully accessible environment for wheelchair users and people with other mobility-related problems.

Design Process

As a result of the brief, the design team created a naturally lit and naturally ventilated facility, thus ensuring that the building is highly cost and energy efficient. During 80 per cent of its intended hours of operation, artificial lighting is not required in the sports hall. Natural light from the north-light roof arrangement is sufficient even on the dullest winter day for playing cricket, and even for televising play.

The new Indoor Cricket Centre also includes Supergrasse Sports Flooring from Australia and specialised rubber shock padding to the bowlers' run-up and follow-through. The nets can be retracted to form either two six-a-side play areas or one large playing hall to ECB standards, and a full-length fast-bowler professional run-up has been included on lane 8. State-of-the-art video and coaching facilities are available in the AV training suite on the top floor. The building houses office accommodation for regional, youth and disabled cricket boards together with changing rooms and toilets, a shop and a top-floor bar with views into the cricket hall and an external terrace.

Wheelchair access is available to reach all parts of the building via an eight-person lift. The changing rooms have tip-up seats to increase manoeuvrability, and the showers have flip-down seats for the disabled. Door openings are wide enough for sports wheelchairs with splayed wheels. Lanes 1 and 8 in the hall are wider than the other lanes to allow greater access and space for the disabled.

It was always the architects' intention to give the building an external appearance that responded to the internal function and to the context which its elevations addressed. During the design process, and in consultation with the city planners, the idea was formed of incorporating a terracotta wall to address the Pershore Road elevation.

At this point the potential of working with artists to create something unique was realised, and Mark Renn and Mick Thacker were approached to join the team to fulfil this goal. Birmingham-based Renn and Thacker had worked with Bryant Priest Newman previously. Since their appointment, the artistic portion of the project gathered considerable momentum and included not only integrated artwork but an external lighting commission, a poetry commission, photography / documentation commission and an education programme run at the Midlands Art Centre (mac). The building is to be the only contemporary structure on Birmingham's Terracotta Trail. Leading artist-photographer Ravi Deepres documented the progress of the cricket centre's construction, as well as all aspects of the arts project.

Project Sign-off

Moss Construction completed the construction of the building within 10 months, and the project finished on budget and on schedule.

The Indoor Cricket Centre won an RIBA Award for Architecture in 2000, a Birmingham Design Initiative Award in 2000, and won the Colourcoat National Building of the Year in 2001 as well as the Innovation category section. The project was the main featured building in the *RIBA Journal* in May 2000 and in *The Architects' Journal* in July 2002.

'This is a low energy, low maintenance building, carefully designed, eminently fit for purpose, and full of thoughtful touches.'
The Architects' Journal, 11 July 2002

The building has been a huge success for the client and is fully booked throughout the autumn and winter months.

'the client is pleased with the finished building, and rightly so.'
RIBA Journal, May 2000

'it was excellent to see Warwickshire's new Indoor Cricket School, it's a fine building and a sign that things may at last be looking up close to home.'
Terry Grimley, *The Birmingham Post*, 14 August 2000

PROJECT TEAM

Client: **Warwickshire County Cricket Club**
Architect: **Bryant Priest Newman Architects with David Morley Architects**
Main Contractor: **Moss Construction Ltd**
Quantity Surveyor: **Francis Graves**
Structural Engineer: **Price & Myers**
Services Engineer: **Max Fordham & Partners**
Planning Supervisor: **Francis Graves**

The Ruskin-inspired Gothic form
and philosophy was respected, and
confusion with new elements avoided by
contemporary treatment.

BIRMINGHAM SCHOOL OF ART
ASSOCIATED ARCHITECTS

Margaret Street, Birmingham

Construction Value: £6.5 million
Completion Date: August 1995

Description

The School of Art is the University of Central England's city-centre base for fine art, sculpture and teaching studies at undergraduate and postgraduate levels. A significant Grade I listed building, it provides a public face for the university with gallery space and a restaurant.

History

The Birmingham Municipal School of Art opened in 1885 as the first municipal art school in the country. Designed by Chamberlain and Martin, it was a pioneering centre offering practical experience in art, crafts and design that influenced art education nationwide. Incorporated into Birmingham Polytechnic and listed in 1971, its status was not matched by funds for maintenance and repair, and by 1990 the building was in poor condition. University status in 1990 delivered funding to repair the building, and an initial programme of external stabilisation and repair was undertaken whilst a comprehensive redevelopment programme was formulated.

Client's Brief

The principal spaces in the school were still suited to contemporary use, but the building did not provide the range of smaller support spaces required by a modern university. The requirements were developed in detail with the department of art and other client groups, and explored in feasibility studies to determine the viability of refurbishment.

The impact of repair and conservation in terms of cost and future flexibility was critical to the university. By the nature of its use, the school needed to be robust and easily maintained: the initial proposals were appraised meticulously against the benchmark of a new building on another site before the design proceeded further.

Design Process

Cleaning and repair were completed between 1990 and 1991, during which time the building was surveyed in detail by the architects. This process was critical in developing a thorough understanding of the building asset.

The principal studios fronting the surrounding streets were still well suited to purpose, and have been restored to their original form by the removal of later subdivisions and surface accretions. Secondary spaces around the internal courtyard were targeted for division to provide a range of spaces for seminars, tutorials and staff offices. Toilets occupying large areas with windows were relocated to more efficient core areas around the two internal lightwells, and large areas of the basement have been reclaimed for sculpture studios. Wood and metal workshops have been grouped together vertically with printing and photography to allow control of the specialist engineering services.

To promote public access a suite of rooms including the library, conference room, exhibition hall and restaurant have been grouped together around the main entrance. A new passenger lift spans the half storey from pavement to ground-floor level, giving access to the entrance hall and security point. Another lift sited in a former lightwell links all floors, culminating in a new second-floor gallery used for visiting exhibitions.

Repair and conservation was a vital part of the project. The Ruskin-inspired Gothic form and philosophy was respected, and confusion with new elements avoided by contemporary treatment, connections making explicit the junction of new and old: the new components were derived from the existing building and related to the overlying grids.

The restoration was thoroughly researched and the fabric repaired as far as possible with similar materials and techniques. Basement waterproofing was accommodated within the thickness of original finishes, with the original materials replaced in position. Paint has everywhere been removed from the finely detailed brick, stone and terracotta.

The original internal decoration was preserved behind later panelling. Walls of studio spaces have been painted in the original pale colours, with the wainscot panelling painted rather than polished to reflect the predilection for white studio space. The principal public areas have been returned to their original condition, complete with furniture and screening.

The entire services installation was unserviceable, with surface-mounted pipework and cabling throughout, and the original heating and ventilation system had been blocked with fire-resisting materials. All the systems have been replaced: heating is with radiators reflecting the Chamberlain and Martin scheme, and ventilation uses sections of the old masonry ducts, with appropriate damping and controls. A full range of power, data, alarm and CCTV services has been integrated with the building fabric, with specialist lighting purpose-designed for the project.

Project Sign-off

The School of Art operated for a century before its refurbishment, and despite a Grade I listed status provided a robust shell able to accommodate significant change. The willingness of the department to challenge accepted relationships between physical space and teaching methods was as critical as the skill of those who originally commissioned, designed and built it, and the school is rightly recognised as a leading institution.

The project was reviewed in *The Architects' Journal* on 16 November 1995. It has received an RIBA Award (1996) and a Civic Trust Award (1998).

PROJECT TEAM

Client: **University of Central England**
Architect: **Associated Architects**
Main Contractor: **Kyle Stewart (Midlands)**
Quantity Surveyor: **Edmond Shipway**
Structural Engineer: **Ove Arup and Partners**
Services Engineer: **H. L. Dawson and Partners**
Specialist Cleaning Consultant: **Adriel**

Quality of environment is an important factor in student choice, and helps the school to attract the best national and international candidates to its courses.

BIRMINGHAM SCHOOL OF JEWELLERY
ASSOCIATED ARCHITECTS

Vittoria Street, Birmingham

Construction Value: £3.8 million
Completion Date: August 1994

MARTINE HAMILTON KNIGHT/BUILTVISION

Description

The School of Jewellery is unique in operating at the heart of Birmingham's Jewellery Quarter, and it offers the broadest curriculum in the UK. Courses include vocational training geared to the local industry as well as undergraduate and postgraduate courses in jewellery, silversmithing, gemmology and horology.

History

The school was founded in 1891 in a Venetian Gothic workshop building of 1862. A further floor was added in 1906, and an extension built in 1911 in an Arts and Crafts style. By the mid-1980s, the school had outgrown its premises and some courses had been relocated to another site; the buildings were in a poor state of repair, the 1911 extension being supported by external scaffolding.

The school separated the various craft disciplines into discrete workshops following traditional industrial practice, making it unsuited to modern teaching and the introduction of new technology. Dirty and dangerous activities requiring close supervision were undertaken throughout the building, with drawing isolated to one remote studio.

A modest adjoining building was offered to the school at this time, giving the possibility of expansion on an enlarged site. With the encouragement of the city council and the jewellery industry, the university embarked on a scheme of redevelopment.

Client's Brief

The new building was to provide accommodation for the students from both the above sites, and to allow for modest expansion. It was critically important that the new spaces should reflect the programme of courses linking traditional craft skills, modern technology and design. The

role of the school in the local industry and community was to be reflected in a range of facilities including exhibition and technical areas, the school playing an active part in industry research and development. In short, the school was to share its life and activity with its neighbours.

Design Process

The new building links the various processes of design and manufacture. By developing communal 'process workshops' for heat and chemical treatment on each floor, the concept of adjoining 'studio workshops' was introduced. Here, both design (at desks) and making (at benches) can take place – supervision being limited to the process workshops, so that students are able to work with hand tools unattended. The sharing of process workshops and the use of glazed partitions encourages interaction between students, and blurs the distinctions between traditional craft skills. The studio workshops are grouped around an atrium, which also links the existing buildings to create a coherent relationship between old and new. This pattern is repeated on four levels, with the corresponding basement space used as a machinery workshop. The simple spatial relationships are echoed in the rational treatment of structure and materials, the atrium resolved in an animated glazed roof. Set aside from the principal activities is a wing containing a restaurant, lecture theatre and seminar rooms.

The process workshops are grouped vertically to control the impact of their high level of services. This allows the studio workshops to be naturally lit and ventilated, using the atrium to generate air movement. Raised floors distribute power, data networks, gas and compressed air to all parts of the building.

The Victorian building was retained in its original form to provide staff accommodation, together with specialist

facilities for horology and gemmology. A large north-lit studio has been retained as exhibition space, and is also used as a jewellery trade centre for the local industry. The restaurant links directly with this space, allowing a range of internal and external events to take place within the school.

The Edwardian annexe was in poor condition – its ground floor set above street level, with spandrel panels obscuring views in. Although larger than the Victorian building it had not displaced the entrance, which, as the central element of the enlarged frontage, took on a new significance. The entrance was re-formed here, stepping the floor down to street level and removing masonry to create a fully glazed, double-height space. The rear half of the building was demolished, the top storey rebuilt and the remaining rooms opened fully to the atrium.

The elevation to the new part of the building is equal in length to the Victorian building and was designed to reflect its scale, balancing the composition around the 1911 annexe. Brick piers and fenestration develop the Edwardian theme, giving expression to the school's history. Clear views into the studio workshops link the internal activity with the street.

Project Sign-off

The building is a direct expression of the UK's leading school of jewellery, and it continues to attract international attention. Quality of environment is an important factor in student choice, and helps the school to attract the best national and international candidates to its courses. It is also a significant urban-regeneration success, which has helped in rejuvenating the Jewellery Quarter and ensuring the continued success of the jewellery industry itself.

The project was reviewed in *The Architects' Journal* on 23 March 1995. It is published in *Birmingham Jewellery Quarter: Architectural Survey of the Manufactories* (English Heritage, 2002), and has received an RIBA Award (1995) and a Civic Trust Award (1996).

PROJECT TEAM

Client: **University of Central England**
Architect: **Associated Architects**
Main Contractor: **Christiani and Neilsen**
Quantity Surveyor: **Edmond Shipway**
Structural Engineer: **Peel and Fowler**
Services Engineer: **H. L. Dawson and Partners**

The structural and mechanical functions were clearly expressed so that visitors could reconcile the magnitudes of scale through an understanding of the building's construction.

MILLENNIUM POINT

GRIMSHAW

Curzon Street, Birmingham

Construction Value: £68.8 million
Completion Date: September 2001

Description

Millennium Point is a world-class centre for technology and learning, and the largest Millennium Project outside London. Set in a 5-hectare former brownfield site, it aims to be a catalyst for the continued regeneration of east Birmingham. The site is within walking distance of Birmingham city centre and adjoins Aston University and the University of Central England's Gosta Green campus.

History

Millennium Point's location is apt, given the West Midlands' proud history of industrial leadership.

The site is bordered by Curzon Street to the south and is adjacent to the listed Curzon Street Station, the terminus for trains arriving from London prior to the development of New Street Station. It is a vast former brownfield area: 5 hectares in total, with the building alone comprising 37,000 m². The site strategy homogenises the internal and external aspects of the scheme. It is based on a single straight pedestrian axis that runs from Curzon Street across the public square, through the building's atrium and out to a landscaped garden adjacent to the Aston University campus. This fulfils the practical requirement of separating visitors from vehicles, dividing the southern square into a pedestrian area to the west and a 750-bay car park to the east.

Client's Brief

Grimshaw were appointed as architects for the project following an interview, and worked to a brief prepared by the city architects and planners in consultation with the tenants: the city's science museum, the University of Central England and the Imax® Corporation. Although the project contract was design-and-build, the client asked Grimshaw to develop the design significantly further than would normally be required of this type of

procurement, and the practice remained in an advisory role throughout the contract, working with the contractor in the development of the building's construction detailing.

An essential aspect of the brief was the creation of a high-quality modern building that is in itself an exercise in innovative technology, effectively becoming part of the educational experience of Millennium Point. The client also wanted a holistic approach: a building in which the structural and mechanical functions were clearly expressed so that visitors could reconcile the magnitudes of scale through an understanding of the building's construction.

Design Process

The plan is organised on the axis of a pedestrian street running from a southern public square through the five-storey atrium of the main building to a landscaped northern garden.

The building comprises two principal elements: the Beam and the Hub. The Beam is a 165 m long by 22 m high composite steel frame and precast concrete structure. It spans east to west across the site and houses the three key components of the project: Thinktank, the Technology Innovation Centre and the University of the First Age. The Beam presents a dual façade to the public square: a full-height, 3 m deep glazed thermal buffer to the east of the entrance, and an independent rain-screen of extruded ceramic louvres to the west.

The Hub is the building's social focus, linking the component parts with commercial facilities on open

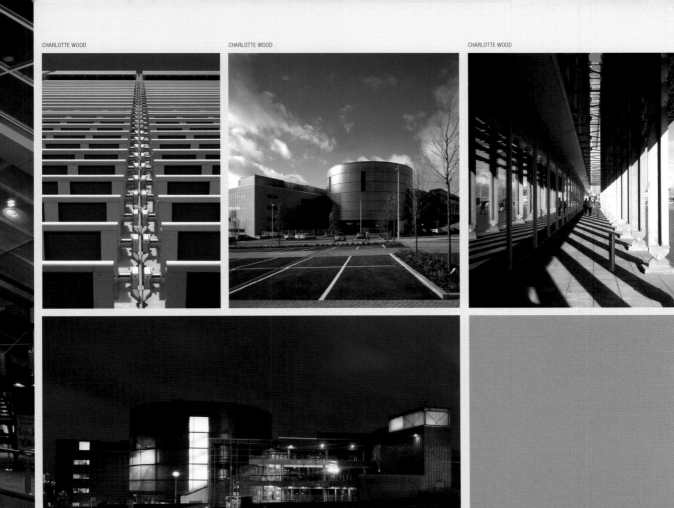

walkways. Its full-height atrium contains the principle vertical circulation for visitors and the dramatic cantilevered form of the region's first Imax® cine-theatre.

Project Sign-off

Millennium Point provided employment for over 3,800 people during construction, and now employs around 500 workers. It is estimated that a further 3,000 people will be employed as a result of the regenerative 'spin-off' effects of the centre, which will include up to £250m of private-sector investment in Eastside over the next ten years.

PROJECT TEAM

Client: **Millennium Point Trust Company Ltd**
Architect: **Grimshaw**
Main Contractor: **Galliford Try**
Quantity Surveyor: **Citex**
Structural Engineer: **Buro Happold**
Services Engineer: **Ove Arup & Partners**

> The architectural solution ... is deliberately strong and invites questioning and debate at various levels – about design, environment, education and expectation.

PERRY BEECHES SCHOOL
URBAN DESIGN BIRMINGHAM CITY COUNCIL

Perry Beeches, Birmingham

Construction Value: £1.4 million
Completion Date: Phase 1: June 1997

Description
A new secondary school in a deprived area of Birmingham.

History
Perry Beeches is a secondary school in the north of Birmingham, whose buildings have been ruined by fire twice in recent years, leaving its staff to teach in a series of isolated temporary huts.

Client's Brief
The brief from the city's Education Department and the school required 'a place of learning and study for young adults with an atmosphere of space, light and tranquillity to encourage and enable personal responsibility from all students including those with disabilities'.

Design Process
The project was to be phased to allow continued occupation during construction. This, the first completed building, provides a flexible arrival, assembly and meeting space; a hall and dining area; administrative and staff offices; and includes a therapy suite and treatment facilities for those requiring specialist assistance during the school day.

The budget of £15m for the whole of the campus was funded by the city's capital allocation and central government's Capital Challenge funding, with the remainder coming through the Public-Private Partnership Initiative. The assembly hub has been funded wholly by the education authority at a total build cost of £1.4m.

The clients responded to the possibility that this first key building of the campus masterplan should set the design standard for the site, with an architectural solution that provided a strong new identity for the school and reflected its emergence from past difficulties into a new and exciting

future. The architectural solution, therefore, is deliberately strong and invites questioning and debate at various levels – about design, environment, education and expectation.

A second teaching area was completed by the same multi-disciplinary team in 1999, and the remainder of the campus was completed by others in 2002 as part of the Public-Private Partnership Initiative.

Design work started in late 1994 and, after an enabling project during 1995, construction of the hub began in April 1996 and was completed in June 1997.

The site slopes down to meet the elevated section of the M6 motorway, and the new building has been built along the east / west contour, to achieve a reasonably consistent floor level. This results in a building with the majority of its spaces facing north or south, making the introduction of high levels of natural lighting more difficult to achieve. It was decided to locate the building such that the entrance took maximum advantage of the shading from the existing copse to the east and appeared to connect to a heavily wooded nature reserve to the west.

The system of interlocking roof planes with deep overhanging eaves and verges has enabled high levels of natural lighting without problems of glare and overheating. The stepped sections also allow for a very efficient system of natural ventilation.

High levels of wall, floor and roof insulation, and thermally broken double glazing all contribute to further minimise energy consumption whilst enhancing the comfort conditions for those using the building. The relatively complex geometry generated by the shading requirements is achieved by a pin-jointed and braced steel frame of either circular or rectangular hollow-section columns.

These support universal-beam rafters with a longitudinal support lattice to the hall, whose top boom extends through to the split prow of the building. The structural frame is exposed throughout and, with the steel staircases and balustrades, is used to punctuate spaces.

The aluminium roof planes and glazing are designed to catch the light differently through the day and offer a subtly varying impact to the primary school and housing higher up the hill. White-rendered walls growing out of planting beds are surmounted either by glazing or white laminate rain-screen panels on a timber sub-frame. Internal partitions are either white-painted impact-resistant plasterboard or naturally stained timber-framed glazing, with the intent to provide a neutral backdrop against which students' work can be exhibited or performed to maximum effect.

The architecture has been described as 'raw and exciting' and 'minimalist, industrial', and it is the use of simple industrial materials that has enabled the variety in space and forms to be achieved within the cost targets.

The aim has been to make a building whose scale is responsive to all those who use the site, from the very youngest children at the nursery to the adults and near-adults at the secondary school.

The internal spaces, their relationships and requirements for volume and light are the generators of the forms, and it is their spatial organisation which has enabled the 'edges' of the building to be kept as low as possible and to grow only in measured slopes and steps away from this critical interface. Apart from the necessary cellular nature of offices and interview rooms, efforts have been made to achieve a series of differentiated yet flowing spaces, intended not to confine the user but to offer a range of ideas and possibilities that raise expectations and encourage creativity.

Project Sign-off

Reaction has been encouraging. Students have been quoted in the press, describing it as 'futuristic', 'like a funfair with roofs you could slide down', 'like magic because it's bigger inside than out' and, significantly, as 'not like a school'.

Staff have been impressed by changes in behaviour generated by the building. Their reactions include: 'pupils are proud of the building and compete to use it', 'their behaviour changes as soon as they come inside' and 'they think it's great'.

Perry Beeches had initially struggled to achieve its target pupil intake, but is now oversubscribed by students and parents placing the school as their first choice.

PROJECT TEAM

Client: **Birmingham City Council – Education Department**
Architect: **Urban Design Birmingham City Council**
Main Contractor: **Willmott Dixon**
Quantity Surveyor: **Urban Design Birmingham City Council**
Structural Engineer: **Urban Design Birmingham City Council**
Services Engineer: **Urban Design Birmingham City Council**
Project Manager: **Urban Design Birmingham City Council**
Planning Supervisor: **Urban Design Birmingham City Council**

LIVING

The revolution in urban living in British cities over the past decade has transformed the way in which we see and experience our urban environment.

For many years Britain set itself apart from the rest of continental Europe by discouraging residential development in its historic city cores. Failed post-war planning policies sought to excessively zone cities and to segregate areas on the basis of uses and functions. The result was city centres that became dead and silent wastelands after people had left work. Birmingham suffered from this problem even more than most other centres, and the problems of zoning were only exacerbated by the disastrous Inner Ring Road development, which cut a swathe through the historic fabric of the city between the 1950s and 1970s. With people discouraged from living centrally, and the Inner Ring Road as an efficient barrier to pedestrian movement, it was hardly surprising that Birmingham's residents were not queuing up to live in the city centre.

Historically, the city had had large working-class neighbourhoods close to the centre. Only slightly further out existed the genteel middle-class suburbs of Edgbaston, Harborne and Moseley. In the post-war era, a concerted effort was made to sweep away the inner working-class districts, which were often needlessly condemned as 'slum housing'. Today, the one remaining example of a row of traditional Birmingham back-to-back workers' housing is owned by the National Trust. It has been lovingly restored and is now, rather ironically, amongst the Trust's most popular holiday rental properties anywhere in the country.

Part-way through the 1990s, Birmingham's attitude to city living began to change. This process was initially quite slow, but has now developed into a full-scale revolution. The first significant scheme to appear was Sherbourne Wharf by Mark Humphries Architects in the mid-1990s. This secluded canalside development was swiftly followed by Crosby Homes' Symphony Court, the first part of the huge Brindleyplace scheme. Crosby Homes had initially been sceptical about the market for city-centre apartments in Birmingham, and had only reluctantly entered into the project. They suspected that many potential buyers would be put off by perceived inner-city problems such as high crime rates and antisocial behaviour. Consequently, Symphony Court was constructed as a walled and gated courtyard development, conveniently surrounded by canal on two sides of its triangular plot. The response to Symphony Court, however, was overwhelming, with most units selling within weeks of release. The city, and Crosby Homes, have not looked back since.

The schemes in this section do not, however, only represent the commercial sector, which is continuing to grow within the city core and surrounding neighbourhoods. Projects such as Ian Simpson's Focus Foyer and Feilden Clegg's Lakeside residences demonstrate how new housing in the city is catering for diverse needs, including the young homeless and the city's burgeoning student population. These projects illustrate how high-quality housing is central to the success of any city seeking to reinvigorate itself at the beginning of the 21st century. With recent developments, such as the stunning Beetham Tower on Holloway Circus, the design bar has been raised higher than ever, and the challenge is growing for other developers to match and exceed these standards. Crosby's Southside and i-land developments on Bromsgrove Street and Urban Splash's rejuvenated Rotunda project are an indication of how this is already beginning to happen.

The Beetham Organization sought to maximise
the potential of a restricted site whilst delivering a
bold, elegant structure which would make a positive
contribution to Birmingham's regeneration.

BEETHAM TOWER

IAN SIMPSON ARCHITECTS

2–18 Holloway Circus, Birmingham

Construction Value: £35.94 million
Completion Date: May 2006

Description

The 122 m high mixed-use tower contains a 220-
bedroom hotel and 152 apartments, including affordable
units, and duplex and penthouse units at the upper levels.
The building forms a striking addition to the Birmingham
skyline and reinforces the significance of a key arrival
point into the city at Holloway Circus.

History

The tower replaced a former low-rise office building on an
extremely tight 1,060 m² site. To the south, it is defined
by the curved pavement edge to the roundabout. As
well as exploiting the footprint and airspace, the building
extends into three levels of basement that accommodate
an automatic stacker system for parking 50 cars.

The initial proposals were for a 192 m tower. However,
owing to the proximity of Birmingham International airport
the Civil Aviation Authority imposed an exclusion height of
122 m, which limited the height of the final design.

Client's Brief

The Beetham Organization sought to maximise
the potential of a restricted site whilst delivering a
bold, elegant structure which would make a positive
contribution to Birmingham's regeneration. The design
had to incorporate the first mixed hotel / residential tower
outside London.

Design Process

The overall design is intended to complement two
adjacent towers in defining Holloway Circus as a
gateway to the city. The hotel component creates an
active presence at street level, continuing the chain of
regeneration along Queensway that links Broad Street and
the Mailbox to New Street Station and the Bullring.

The exterior skin reinforces the verticality of the tower. Its
sculptural form has a unity which is greater than the sum
of the functions it encloses. The façade emphasises this
unity rather than the traditional modernist approach of
articulating the building structure or sections with different
materials.

The envelope consists of three distinct façade treatments
which retain the effect of a seamless skin. They respond
to the context and orientation of the site and address the
rigorous performance requirements for energy-efficiency
and solar gain. A combination of panels and composite
units, some glass-clad and the remainder clear glazed,
covers the east and west elevations. To the north, staggered
textured stainless-steel panelling encloses the two stair
cores and contrasts with the glazing used elsewhere.
Between the cores, the façade is a random arrangement of
stainless-steel-clad and clear glazed panels, with the extent
of transparency increasing at the higher residential levels.

The dominant south façade is smooth, curved and
completely glazed, following the site boundary along
Holloway Circus. Here, the skin is composed of unitised
panels with a series of glass treatments – clear glazing,
a fritted turquoise pattern, vertical fritted blue stripes,
horizontal opening glass-louvre blades and perforated
stainless-steel panels which conceal inward-opening
ventilation slots. Whilst performing a significant role in the
envelope's solar control, the frit patterns also introduce a
sense of vitality with colour to the building's environment,
and a playful interaction of sunlight and shadow internally.

On the residential levels, banks of manually openable
glass louvres shield enclosed balconies to the south-
facing apartments, creating a feeling of airiness and
space for the occupants. The variable arrangement of
louvres animates the otherwise taut skin of glass.

The first 19 floors of the tower accommodate the hotel, with the main public areas and their associated support facilities, such as kitchens, occupying the full footprint of the site. Above these lower podium levels the tower adopts its slender form, which continues over the hotel-bedroom levels and the majority of the residential floors.

The head of the tower is articulated firstly by a continuous stainless-steel lined 'shadow gap', followed by the cantilevering of the upper levels forward of the main façade line, providing a penthouse belvedere with uninterrupted views towards the Malvern Hills. The treatment of this façade defines a sculptural element with a strong horizontality, which is in contrast to the vertical expression of the remainder of the tower. The east, west and north elevations are enclosed in white glass-clad composite panels and clear glazing. To the south, continuous banks of horizontal glass louvres serve full-width winter gardens. The two north-facing stair cores are finished with stainless-steel spires, which further enhance the tower's profile.

Project Sign-off

Beetham Tower is a sculptural object defining a new positive identity for an otherwise unprepossessing ring-road site. It is symbolic of the ambition of Birmingham's ongoing regeneration. The façade offers glimpses of the activity within, but the building form belies the domestic scale of its accommodation. As one approaches, its scale expands from slender to monumental and its sleek skin unveils the complexity of its construction and glazing treatments.

Ian Simpson says, 'I am passionate about high-density living and brownfield parts of a city. We took a prosaic system of accommodation and used it to start thinking about how to create a building that contributes to the city.'

PROJECT TEAM

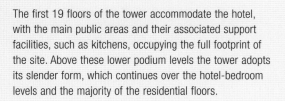

Client: **Beetham Organization**
Architect: **Ian Simpson Architects**
Main Contractor: **Laing O'Rourke Midlands**
Cost Manager: **Qubed**
Structural Engineer: **WSP Group**
Services Engineer: **Buro Happold**
Planning Supervisor: **OME Ltd**
Fire Consultant: **Arup Fire**
Acoustic Consultant: **AEC**
Lighting Consultant: **Maurice Brill Lighting Design**

> Foyers provide a safe and secure environment for a mix of people from differing backgrounds and in different situations.

FOCUS FOYER

IAN SIMPSON ARCHITECTS

St Chad's Circus, Birmingham

Construction Value: £3.3 million
Completion Date: May 1998

Description

The Focus Foyer provides accommodation for young people between the ages of 16 and 25, and acts as a resource centre providing training and education facilities for residents and other young locals. The six-storey building is located adjacent to St Chad's Circus roundabout, opposite the Roman Catholic cathedral.

History

Ian Simpson Architects won an international design competition in March 1993 for the design of the UK's first purpose-built Foyer – a competition organised and sponsored by the Architecture Foundation, the Housing Corporation and Shelter. Shape Housing Association, which subsequently became part of Focus Housing Group, had won a parallel national competition in 1992 to build the Foyer and had subsequently worked with the Housing Corporation and Shelter to develop the design-competition brief for a site in Birmingham.

Client's Brief

Foyers provide a safe and secure environment for a mix of people from differing backgrounds and in different situations, including students as well as workers and the unemployed. The average stay is between 6 and 18 months, rents are low and unemployed residents have to commit to undertake training. The aim is to help young people break the 'no home, no job' cycle.

The design brief was to provide 80 bedrooms with en suite facilities, together with communal kitchens on each floor; a residents' restaurant, resource room, IT suite, meeting room and laundry; staff offices; and 13 car parking spaces.

Design Process

The extended time taken between the competition and final start on site (a period of four years in total) was due to a number of factors including changes in site, client, brief, budget and design team.

The original competition site was wedged between a tall building, a canal and a viaduct, and located on a quiet narrow street. During the scheme-design process, an intensive period of redesign was undertaken which reduced the Foyer in scale. Despite this reduction in scale, the design team were subsequently advised that development could not take place within a certain distance of the railway viaduct – and this effectively ruled out development on the competition site.

The original client, Shape, was taken over by another housing association, Focus, who entered into negotiations with the city to buy a different site: a very prominent, open, city-centre plot on a busy ring-road roundabout.

The city was keen to have a landmark building on the new site, which is effectively a gateway to the city centre. The building was designed to wrap around the edge of the site, following the curve of the road and reinforcing the form of the recently remodelled St Chad's Circus. This creates a peaceful, landscaped courtyard to the rear, which is overlooked by the bedrooms. The entrance to the building is from this courtyard, creating a feeling of safety and security and reinforcing the private nature of a 'residence'. The restaurant, meeting rooms and training rooms at ground-floor level act as a window to the local community and provide a transitional zone between the street and the four private bedroom floors above. Stairs and a lift give access to a broad single-banked corridor, which provides both communal and circulation space with views out onto the busy street below and the city centre beyond, or, if the resident chooses, interaction and communication with the bedroom itself. This corridor also acts as an acoustic buffer, protecting the bedrooms from the noise of the traffic. Disabled bedrooms are integrated within each floor.

The elevations reflect the internal organisation. The distinction between the public areas on the ground floor and the more private bedroom / living accommodation above is clearly articulated in the change of materials and in the arrangement of the fenestration. The simple monolithic form of the building called for very crisp detailing and careful selection of materials. The red brickwork is designed to make clear that it is not load-bearing but is a series of cladding panels set within the expressed steel-framed structure. The setting out and detailing of the building has been carefully considered and executed to achieve this. The bays of stretcher bond brickwork, separated by the horizontal banding of the articulated floor beams and vertical slot windows, are divided up further with both recessed vertical joints coinciding with the steel columns on the street side and the bedroom walls on the courtyard side, and recessed horizontal joints, aligning with the window sills and transoms.

Project Sign-off

Ian Simpson Architects worked on the Focus Foyer over a number of years, with the aim of producing a building that reflects the intentions of the original competition-winning scheme despite changes in site, brief, budget, client and design team. The building was successfully completed in May 1998. It displays a rigour and integrity which results from the commitment of all parties, particularly the client, together with the determination of the design team and contractor. The building has won a number of awards, including a Housing Design Award and a Civic Trust Award.

ALL IMAGES ON THIS SPREAD MARTINE HAMILTON KNIGHT/BUILTVISION

PROJECT TEAM

Client: **Focus Housing Group**
Architect: **Ian Simpson Architects**
Main Contractor: **Moss Construction**
Quantity Surveyor: **Silk & Frazier**
Structural Engineer: **Maurice Johnson & Associates**
Services Engineer: **Powerline**
Project Manager: **Cyril Sweet Project Consultants**
Planning Supervisor: **Walker Cotter**

Lakeside Residences provides
accommodation for 651 students on a tight
urban site in central Birmingham, only a
short walk from the main shopping areas.

LAKESIDE RESIDENCIES, ASTON UNIVERSITY

FEILDEN CLEGG BRADLEY ARCHITECTS LLP

Aston Triangle, Birmingham

Construction Value: £14.24 million
Completion Date: August 1999

Description

The scheme provides over 600 student apartments on a
tight urban site. Flats are arranged in two blocks running
north–south to ensure good daylighting in all rooms.

History

The building plot was a brownfield site that had been
developed since the early 19th century for a variety
of industrial uses, although immediately prior to this
development it had been used as the university overspill
car park.

Feilden Clegg Bradley Architects were appointed as lead
design consultants, following a competitive interview
process, in November 1996. Lakeside Residences
provides accommodation for 651 students on a tight
urban site in central Birmingham, only a short walk from
the main shopping areas and on the edge of the university
campus. The scheme replaced older off-campus rooms
located about four miles away.

Designs were worked up for a planning application
submitted in June 1997. A two-stage selection tendering
procedure led to the appointment of John Laing
Construction as main contractor in September of that year,
with a start being made on site in early 1998.

Client's Brief

The site is adjacent to the Inner Ring Road and the
scheme was developed to suit the proposed alterations
to create a tree-lined boulevard circumnavigating the
city centre.

The scheme follows the model set down in the university
brief for groups of between six and ten en suite bedrooms
sharing kitchen / dining / living facilities. A variety of flat
and maisonette plans was developed, all based upon a
similar study-bedroom layout.

Careful consideration was given to buildability,
incorporating prefabricated bathroom pods to meet an
ambitious construction timetable.

Design Process

The scheme comprises flats of between six and ten
en suite bedrooms sharing kitchen, dining and living
facilities. They range from 4 to 16 storeys in height and
occupy two blocks running north–south to ensure good
daylighting in all rooms. The city-centre scale is picked
up in the western block with a sinuous eight-storey wall
to the Inner Ring Road, which terminates in a 16-storey
tower providing a landmark for the university at its main
vehicular entry point. The eastern block draws on the
scale of the lower-rise campus buildings, with a four-
storey terrace overlooking the existing lake, terminating in
a nine-storey tower at its southern end.

Between these two 'limbs' is a linear courtyard, which
opens to the south providing a strong sense of enclosure
and community, and forming the focus of activity for the
scheme. The courtyard terminates at its northern end in
a reception building which marks the main pedestrian
access to the campus from the city centre. This pavilion
provides security and administrative facilities both for
students and for conference delegates. All front doors are
accessed from the courtyard, and living rooms at lower
levels open on to it. Upper-level living rooms face out to
the James Watt Queensway and, on the eastern side, to
the landscaped heart of the campus.

The primary structure comprises in situ concrete walls
and slabs based on a module of two bedroom bays. Pre-
finished concrete bathroom units are provided to ensure a
high-quality finish throughout. Externally, the scheme

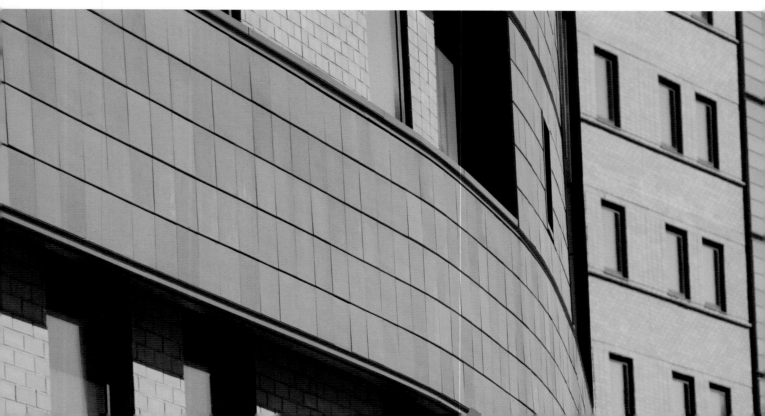

combines terracotta brickwork, supported over the frame, with a terracotta rain-screen cladding which emphasises the linearity of the elevations. Windows are grouped in slots within the rain-screen, and upper-level living rooms form recessed bays which give onto balconies overlooking the street. The top storey is set back and clad with dark insulated render, and a continuous, sinuous aluminium roof falls to a central gutter.

The scheme has been designed to minimise energy usage, with high levels of insulation throughout and heat-reclamation ventilation systems. The project is intended to have energy consumption as low as, or lower than, any equivalent scheme in Britain.

Project Sign-off

A high density of development has been achieved, with a floor area of 15,964 m^2 on a 7,921 m^2 site – representing a plot ratio of over 2:1. This ratio is significantly higher than comparable university-sector housing.

A cooperative team spirit was encouraged between consultants and contractor, which led to an out-turn contract value of £14.2 m being agreed several months before practical completion. Completion was achieved on time in August 1999, and students took up residence for the start of the 1999 academic year at the end of September.

PROJECT TEAM

Client: **Aston University**
Architect: **Feilden Clegg Bradley Architects LLP**
Main Contractor: **John Laing Construction Ltd**
Quantity Surveyor: **Faithful+Gould**
Structural Engineer: **Buro Happold**
Services Engineer: **Buro Happold**
Project Manager: **EC Harris**
Landscape Consultants: **Teasdale Environmental Design**

It is built on a single large urban block, but has been broken into two very distinct elements with a new 12 m wide public thoroughfare running through the middle of the development.

SOUTHSIDE AND I-LAND
GLENN HOWELLS ARCHITECTS

Bromsgrove Street, Birmingham

Construction Value: £32 million
Completion Date: Ongoing

Description

Glenn Howells Architects are working on several residential projects in the Bromsgrove Street area, giving them a unique opportunity to create a unifying approach to the development of this part of the city.

The first completed development is Southside, a mixed-use scheme providing 180 apartments over street-level commercial / retail space. The next phase is i-land, which rises to ten storeys at the prominent corner of Bromsgrove and Essex Streets.

History

The site lies close to the historic markets quarter of Birmingham and the emerging entertainment district around Hurst Street and China Town.

Until the Second World War this site was home to densely packed back-to-back housing, which was later almost entirely replaced by small-scale commercial premises. The sole exception was the corner of Hurst Street and Inge Street, where several back-to-back houses (which have since received Grade II status) have been refurbished by the Birmingham Conservation Trust.

Immediately to the north of the site lies the Birmingham Hippodrome Theatre, which has been at the heart of the city's cultural life since 1899. This has also undergone major refurbishment in recent times.

Prior to redevelopment the site was used as a surface car park.

Client's Brief

Crosby Homes (Special Projects) recognised the potential of this site as a large area of redundant land in the heart of the city centre – offering both the opportunity of a

CROSBY LEND LEASE

ROD DORLING

ROD DORLING

development plot in its own right, and a catalyst for the future regeneration of this part of the city.

The area is home to a range of lively pubs, clubs and restaurants focused on Hurst Street. However, it currently lacks residential units.

The client's brief sought to rectify this imbalance, introducing city living into Southside while transforming this underused site and creating a dense urban fabric reminiscent of the area's historic street pattern.

It was felt that the high quality of residential accommodation required, combined with the provision of public and private spaces, should be respectful of the historic context while improving pedestrian links from the city centre.

Car parking was to be provided to a level of approximately 70 per cent, with minimal impact on the surrounding environment. Activity was encouraged through shops and bars at street level.

Design Process

Southside is a mixed-use scheme providing 180 one- and two-bed apartments above commercial / retail space at street level, with basement car parking and landscaped courtyards. The scheme is notable for the way in which it has introduced a new 'street' across the middle of the site. It is built on a single large urban block, but has been broken into two very distinct elements with a new 12 m wide public thoroughfare running through the middle of the development. This innovation allowed the developer to achieve higher densities and maximise the commercial potential of the site, while breaking down the potentially overbearing scale of the scheme. The new thoroughfare is an unusual feature for such a development, and it adds to the street-level interest and activity of the area. Ground-floor uses along Hurst Street and Bromsgrove Street are mainly retail.

The adjacent i-land development, also by Glenn Howells Architects for Crosby Homes, is an imposing corner building drawing influences from New York's Flatiron building of 1902. The scheme, which is slightly higher than the adjacent Southside, aims to articulate the Essex Street / Bromsgrove Street junction as a major urban nexus and help restore Bromsgrove Street's status as a significant urban artery. At the corner, the building is terminated in distinctive curved glazed windows, adding a sense of drama to an otherwise restrained but sophisticated architectural composition. An internal courtyard provides a communal focus with a strong curved form and an extensive use of water.

Project Sign-off

Southside and i-land demonstrate that mass-commercial / urban-residential schemes can contribute to high-quality urban design. They also show that commercial pressures for high densities need not compromise design quality. Indeed, Southside and i-land inject a strong and confidently urban design sense into a neglected part of Birmingham. Glenn Howells Architects are working on a number of other schemes in the vicinity, and aim to add to the growing architectural coherency of this street. In the long term, the practice's ambition is to see Bromsgrove Street restored to its full historic length, with rebuilding on the redeveloped wholesale markets site.

PROJECT TEAM

Client: **Beetham Organization**
Client: **Crosby Homes (Special Projects)**
Architect: **Glenn Howells Architects**
Main Contractor: **Taylor Woodrow**
Quantity Surveyor: **Back Group**
Structural Engineer: **Scott Wilson Kirkpatrick & Co Ltd**
Services Engineer: **Hoare Lea**
Project Manager: **Crosby Homes (Special Projects)**
CDM Coordinator: **Not yet appointed**

The Rotunda is a Grade II listed structure dating from the early 1960s, and one of Birmingham's most recognisable landmarks.

THE ROTUNDA
GLENN HOWELLS ARCHITECTS

150 New Street, Birmingham

Construction Value: £21 million
Completion Date: February 2008

Description

The Rotunda redevelopment proposals involve conversion of the 22-storey office tower into 234 high-quality apartments, in the process restoring its iconic status. Proposals also include a double-height entrance and a new building 'skin' using differing, textured glass panels to deliver energy-efficiency, maximise views and transform the appearance of the building's powerful, cylindrical form.

History

The Rotunda is a Grade II listed structure dating from the early 1960s, and one of Birmingham's most recognisable landmarks. It is situated within the newly redeveloped Bullring shopping centre – the new heart of Birmingham city-centre retail – close to New Street Station, and is well placed to continue this part of the city centre regeneration.

The physical constraints – such as the limited floor-to-floor heights, load-bearing capacity and the radial footprint – render it inappropriate for modern office requirements. The proposed transformation to residential use was therefore considered an ideal solution to ensure the long-term future of the building.

Client's Brief

Developer Urban Splash has an unrivalled reputation for delivering quality, design-led and award-winning schemes.

The objective was to build on this and to adopt a design approach to retain and enhance the iconic quality of the building, delivering a residential component that respects the landmark and continues to provide a visual marker on the city's skyline.

Design Process

The existing Rotunda is cylindrical in shape and rises approximately 80 m above street level, with a diameter of 32 m and an inner central core 14 m in diameter. There are 36 perimeter columns, spaced at 2.8 m apart.

In respect of its technical performance, the original façade was failing in a number of places and it was therefore proposed to develop a new bespoke prefabricated curtain-walling system that complements the inherent form of the building and is arranged on the existing facet of five degrees, giving 72 glazed modules.

Views out are currently limited by the mid-height spandrel panels, and therefore the design concept for the façade is to replace these with full-height glazing which will greatly improve external awareness and provide high levels of transparency.

On every pair of facets, it is proposed that one glazing module is fixed and the other is an internal sliding door that sits flush into the façade and steps in to slide across, like an airliner's door. With an internal glazed balustrade and consistency in appearance between fixed and opening lights, the smoothness and simplicity of the elevation is preserved.

The materials proposed for the curtain-wall system comprise an anodised aluminium frame enclosing high-performance glass that does not compromise transparency; and textured white opaque glass for the spandrel panel, giving a reflective quality similar to the existing mosaic tiles.

The contrast between spandrel panels and clear glazing is retained as a principal characteristic of the horizontal banding on the existing façade, which is identified in the listing documents.

With full-height glazing, it is also proposed there is some control and consistency in the surface treatment for

space. An uninterrupted ramp, finished in the same granite flooring as the square, seamlessly leads the visitor in to the central core.

To reflect the character of the existing podium, the white marble mosaics on the external cladding are also continued inside for the proposed wall finishes to the entrance foyer.

The existing office circulation, comprising five passenger lifts and two staircases, sits within the central concrete core. For residential use, it is proposed to rationalise the core layout to provide an attractive lobby entrance and create new openings in the core structure to access the apartments. The reconfigured core will incorporate two new passenger lifts sitting within the existing lift shafts, and the retention of one of the staircases.

Project Sign-off

Despite recent nearby arrivals the Rotunda remains Birmingham's key landmark tower, and its design-led 'face-lift' will not only ensure the long-term future of this Grade II structure but will also significantly enhance the image of the city.

There has been overwhelming support from Birmingham's citizens and council representatives for the transformation of the Rotunda into a quality landmark. The intensive design process between client and design team should ensure the success of the project, restoring a much-loved icon to its rightful place on Birmingham's skyline.

Work on demolition and modifications to the existing structure commenced in late 2005, with completion of the project expected early in 2008.

window 'dressing' to provide privacy and shading. Bespoke blinds or screens will therefore form part of the fit-out for the apartments, and are currently being developed.

The lighting proposal for the top of the building is key to the visual quality of this landmark, and it is therefore proposed to replace the existing top band with a lightbox structure that maintains the existing proportions of the cylindrical form. Opportunities for colour, movement and signage are currently being considered as part of the lighting strategy.

The Rotunda will house 234 apartments on 18 floors. On a typical floor, the party walls radiate from the central-core wall to align with the perimeter columns. As a result, there are three primary types of apartment – Citypad, one-bedroom and two-bedroom apartments, covering two, three and four bays respectively.

Sitting just below the lightbox band, the top floor houses six penthouses with private balcony spaces. The existing 'shadow-gap' feature is retained to help announce the distinct top to the building and to provide the balcony space. This level also offers a column-free space with unobstructed views across the cityscape.

Careful consideration has been given to the internal planning of the segment-shaped apartments. A concentric approach for the arrangement of spaces has located bathrooms and kitchens towards the central core, allowing the habitable spaces to enjoy maximum access to daylight and views out.

At the base, the existing reception area will be reconfigured to create a greater presence on the approach from the urban square. On arrival, a double-height single-glazed screen invites the visitor into a dramatic foyer

PROJECT TEAM

Client: **Urban Splash**
Architect: **Glenn Howells Architects**
Main Contractor: **Urban Splash Build**
Cost Consultant: **Simon Fenton Partnership**
Structural Consultant: **Dewhurst Macfarlane & Partners**
Services Consultant: **Buro Happold**
Project Manager: **Gardiner & Theobald**
Façade Consultant: **Wintech**
Acoustic Consultant: **R W Gregory**

Snow Hill Station was opened in 1852 on the Great Western Railway line from London Paddington to Wolverhampton, and was remodelled several times over the following century.

SNOW HILL
GLENN HOWELLS ARCHITECTS

Snow Hill, Queensway, Birmingham

Construction Value: £90 million
Completion Date: July 2010

Description

Part of the larger Snow Hill development, this mixed-use residential, hotel and commercial project includes basement car parking and a new landscaped public realm. It comprises two aluminium-and-glass-clad towers, the hotel tower rising 23 storeys and the residential one 42 storeys (260 m) in height. They are linked at lower levels and by a bridge framing a public route through the site.

History

Snow Hill Station was opened in 1852 on the Great Western Railway line from London Paddington to Wolverhampton, and was remodelled several times over the following century. During the 1960s, it was declared surplus to requirements and was recommended for closure. All services were redirected to New Street Station and, despite a huge public outcry, its much-loved Great Western Hotel was demolished in 1969 – followed by the rest of the station in 1977. Ambitious redevelopment plans failed to materialise, and by the mid-1980s British Rail decided to reopen Snow Hill as part of Birmingham's cross-city transport plan. In 1987, the newly rebuilt station opened for services to the south only. Generally regarded as an unworthy successor to the old station, the new Snow Hill has been widely criticised as draughty, unwelcoming and architecturally unimaginative.

Since the completion of the Inner Ring Road, the site adjacent to the station has been left as a surface car park. The accompanying system of pedestrian underpasses resulted in a hostile public realm and poor connections from the city centre to the historic Gun Quarter and A. W. N. Pugin's nearby St Chad's Cathedral.

Client's Brief

The brief was developed from Birmingham City Council's 2002 Development Brief for the Snow Hill site. Ballymore

/ RT Group Developments acquired the site from Railtrack and entered into a number of Section 106 obligations, including realignment of the road network. This removed the 'concrete collar' of the existing ring road, improved opportunities for pedestrian links and the public realm, and created an enlarged development site adjacent to Snow Hill Station.

The masterplan, prepared by Sidell Gibson Architects, developed key principles with reference to BCC's Masterplanning Brief for the site and other planning guidance. Planning negotiations were held with BCC throughout the process.

Glenn Howells Architects were engaged by Ballymore to develop Building 3 at the northern end of the site, working closely with SGA and BCC in the process.

Key Principles:

- Align commercial and urban masterplanning objectives by creating lively mixed-use frontages, which integrate buildings into the urban scene.

- Improve street connectivity and urban grain, and increase pedestrian permeability through the site.

- Introduce high-quality amenity space and emphasise the quality of urban design.

- Provide a high standard of flexible commercial and residential accommodation designed for sustainability.

- Create a legible urban environment, which marks the edge of the city centre from the north and west and extends the sequence of public squares.

The development includes a new square adjoining St Chad's Cathedral, a square adjoining Colmore Row and

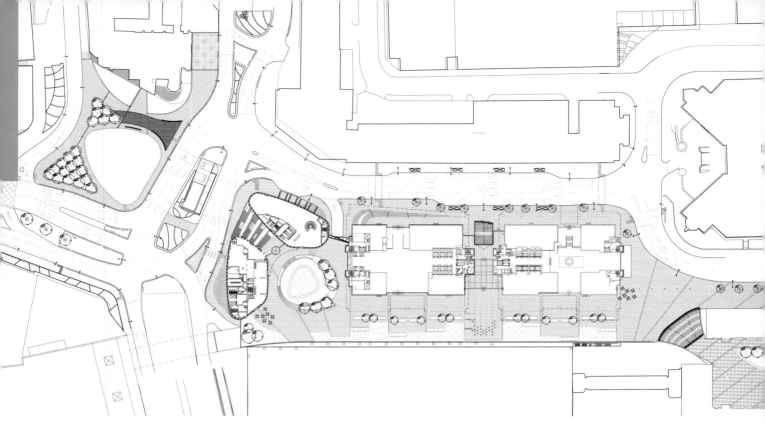

Snow Hill Station itself, and a pedestrian route through the site which also allows for the proposed extension of the Midland Metro light-rail service.

Design Process

Each end of the Snow Hill site was identified in the BCC 'High Places' publication (published 2003) as being suitable for a tall building.

The concept for two towers of different heights framing a pedestrian route through the site was felt to provide the best urban-design response, both to the site and to the client's requirements. The plan allows the shape of the buildings to address the street, and also to accommodate a new public space and route within the development.

A number of configurations for two separate towers were drawn and modelled, and the effect of the building massing, long-range views, public realm and urban grain, solar orientation and other environmental factors were considered for each.

Two similar curving plan forms were developed, enclosing a new square public space and framing a diagonal route towards St Chad's Cathedral.

The stepped pedestrian route between the towers forms a symbolic gateway to the development, and addresses the 7 m change of level on site. The massing of the sequence of buildings step up in height gradually, culminating in the 42-storey residential tower which addresses the new open space to the north (St Chad's Square) and the approaches from the north of the city.

Each of the towers has a relatively small floorplate, and the buildings therefore achieve a very slender and elegant profile. The detailed design concentrated on achieving a simple and distinctive built form with a clearly defined base, middle and top.

The plan shape of each tower is based on complementary curving forms (related to the shape of the site boundary). Solar orientation of the towers was considered, together with the impact on adjacent public spaces. Wind-tunnel modelling, which was carried out during the design-development stage, demonstrated a beneficial effect from the proposed development on the environment around Snow Hill, and identified areas in which additional screening and planting were required.

Accommodation / interior layout

The residential building accommodates over 330 apartments, and the hotel will be 5-star with 170 bedrooms. The towers are linked at Level 1 by a bridge accommodating the hotel bar and restaurant. Leisure and conference facilities and other uses ancillary to the hotel, together with 180 parking spaces, are located below the landscaped square and in the basement levels.

Active frontages are provided at podium level and street level.

Site/landscape

The continuation of safe and pleasant pedestrian routes through the site, and the creation of high-quality public space, was fundamental to the design development and the aspirations of the masterplan. All vehicle circulation and servicing for the entire site occurs below the podium / viaduct, creating a car-free pedestrian realm throughout the development.

A new square is created, enclosed on two sides by the towers and enlivened by active uses (cafés, hotel entrance and commercial units) at ground-floor level. High-quality landscaping in this space will include a water-wall feature, tree planting and a lawned central space suitable for public events. The landscaping of this

square is part of a sequence of spaces considered by the overall landscape strategy for the site, which includes the use of high-quality granite paving.

A range of shapes and façade treatments was considered for the building elevations. For practical and aesthetic reasons a lightweight metal-and-glass façade was chosen, with projecting 'fins' to the mullions and transoms to provide a high degree of depth and surface articulation. A regular module is proposed, with the mullions at alternate wide and narrow spacings. The narrow panel provides ventilation in the residential tower, or is a fixed metal-faced panel in the hotel block. The two towers therefore have the same architectural language but achieve a slightly different appearance, with greater solidity to the shorter hotel tower and a finer grain and 'lighter' appearance to the residential tower.

Hand-drawn sketches, computer visuals, animation and physical modelling at various scales (up to 1:10) were used throughout the process to examine the appearance of the elevation options and to assess internal and external views. The client also built full-size mock-ups of the apartment layouts to assess the quality of the internal spaces and the effect of the façades on the internal appearance of the units.

Within a regular façade module, large full-height fixed glass panels provide excellent views from the apartments, and alternate slender insulated opening panels provide natural ventilation. Structural columns are faced with glazed shadow boxes, providing a uniform appearance to the upper parts of the towers. At the lower three levels, the increased storey heights and the introduction or omission of a solid infill panel to the paired mullions shows the structure more clearly and expresses a larger architectural order. At street level, the metal façade comes down to bear on a solid pre-cast concrete plinth.

Project Sign-off

Liaison with Birmingham City Council throughout the design-development process was reciprocated with good support. There has also been a positive dialogue with nearby St Chad's Cathedral.

Construction is due to start on site in July 2007. It is anticipated that all phases of the development will be completed during 2010.

PROJECT TEAM

Client: **Ballymore Properties Ltd**
Architect: **Glenn Howells Architects**
Main Contractor: **CSL**
Quantity Surveyor: **Gleeds**
Structural Engineer: **WSP**
Services Engineer: **Hoare Lea**
Project Manager: **CSL**
Interior Architect/Designer: **Johnson Naylor**

PUBLIC REALM

The reinvention of Birmingham over the past two decades began principally in its streets and squares. When the city council set about the development of the new convention centre in the mid-1980s, they soon realised that prestigious buildings would not be enough in themselves to attract people back to the city.

What was needed was a complete overhaul of the public realm – the streets and spaces that lay languishing between the city's buildings, and which had been neglected for so long. The first of these new spaces to be created was Centenary Square, a dream of the city's planners for decades that was finally made possible by the building of the ICC. What followed was nothing less than a total transformation in the way that the city perceived itself. The feeble and localised pedestrianisation schemes of the 1980s were replaced with a far more radical and bolder vision, in which the pedestrian finally regained supremacy over the car. These changes went hand in hand with a fundamental reassessment of the Inner Ring Road. Once seen as the answer to Birmingham's problems, by the early 1980s it was increasingly realised that the ring road was effectively 'strangling' the city centre and restricting growth. The consequences had been disastrous, with people discouraged from moving across (or rather under) this huge road via its intimidating underpasses. At Centenary Square, Tess Jaray's paved footbridge seamlessly links the central library to the whole Broad Street area and beyond. What was once a remote hinterland has become a focal point of an expanding and vibrant city centre.

BELOW AND BACKGROUND IMAGE PATEL TAYLOR   CRAIG HOLMES/IMAGES OF BIRMINGHAM

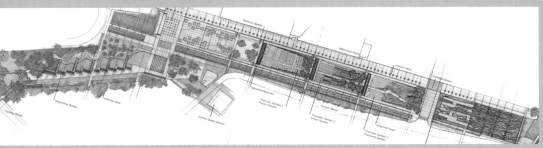

Following from this early success came the acclaimed Victoria Civic Square collaboration between the city's own Landscape Practice Group and the Gujarati-born Royal Academician and renowned sculptor, Dhruva Mistry. Victoria Civic Square reinvented what had been a barren patch of grass and turned it into a fitting foreground to Yeoville Thomason's Council House and Hansom and Welch's outstanding 19th-century Town Hall. The clever mix of classical European civic space with Indian-influenced statuary is a delightful and highly successful gesture towards recognising the complex ethnic mix that represents contemporary Birmingham. Elsewhere in the city, numerous other public spaces have been revamped, recreated or made from scratch. Most notable are Townshend Landscape's series of squares at Brindleyplace and Gross Max's new St Martin's Square at the Bullring – both dealt with elsewhere in this book.

Now, as the city expands even further beyond the artificial constraints once imposed by the ring road, the council are planning the most ambitious new public space in over a century. Patel Taylor's new City Park in Eastside promises to be outstanding. It will link what are currently a number of disparate elements in the Eastside quarter and create a new green lung, reaching into the heart of the city. The hope is that the park will not only spur further regeneration, but that it will act as a vital place of refuge in an increasingly bustling and thriving city.

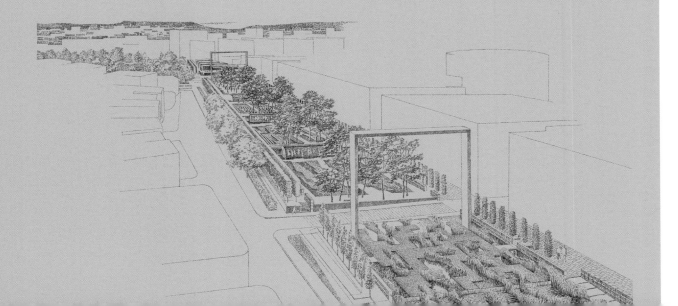

The civic centre, where Centenary Square is now located, has always been an important location, and during the early 20th century ambitious plans were proposed to create a grand plaza with adjoining exhibition halls.

CENTENARY SQUARE
BIRMINGHAM DESIGN SERVICES

Broad Street, Birmingham

Construction Value: £3.1 million
Completion Date: June 1991

Description

The civic square adjoining the International Convention Centre was opened in 1991 and named to mark Birmingham's centenary as a city in 1989. This important inner-city open space integrates into its design a combination of hard and soft elements with several formal works of art. The space provides a variety of functions including the capacity to stage large-scale organised events.

History

The civic centre, where Centenary Square is now located, has always been an important location, and during the early 20th century ambitious plans were proposed to create a grand plaza with adjoining exhibition halls. Although these were later abandoned on cost grounds, its location would always ensure this area's fundamental importance in the heart of the city.

In the 1960s, much of the surrounding area fell into decay and the construction of the Inner Ring Road created a 'concrete collar', making it increasingly difficult for pedestrians to freely move through Birmingham's centre.

To reverse the damaging trends of the past, Birmingham City Council recognised the need for a bold development programme which would reinvent the city's image, making it a desirable place in which to live and work.

Work began in 1988, in parallel with the construction of the International Convention Centre, and funding was set aside for the development of the building's forecourt. At the time, the square was laid out as gardens to the Hall of Memory, with grassed areas, flower beds, a fountain and footpaths leading up to a stone colonnade. As the plan to redevelop the city's image unfolded, the opportunity arose to create a unique civic square.

PAUL WARD/IMAGES OF BIRMINGHAM

Client's Brief

The challenge was to create a new civic square that would become a significant urban centre for social activity. The key points of the client's brief stated that the plan must:

- form an important pedestrian link to the city centre, which could accommodate peak flows likely to be generated from the National Indoor Arena and the International Convention Centre;

- develop a multi-functional space that continues in its role of being an area for informal recreation as well a place in which to stage significant organised events;

- provide a sense of arrival by forming an entranceway to the International Convention Centre;

- respond to the scale and character both of new and existing buildings adjacent to the site;

- provide both hard and soft landscape elements, with adequate provision for sitting-out and with special attention to the choice of street furniture to provide additional character;

- incorporate a planting scheme that offers year-round interest;

- consider how vacant sites adjoining the square may be treated in the future.

Design Process

The development of Centenary Square began in 1989 with the construction of Centenary Way: the first bridge to stretch across the Inner Ring Road, which created an uninterrupted pedestrian route from the city centre to the civic square.

The existing garden contained the city's main war memorials, some of which were incorporated into the new design. The colonnade which formerly stood in the garden was moved to the nearby St Thomas's Peace Garden, where it now houses many plaques containing messages of peace from around the world. The domed Hall of Memory still remains: a landmark feature at the east end of Centenary Square, giving the space a strong sense of historical continuity.

The design process also required the careful collection and exhibition of several contemporary pieces of public art. This included *The Spirit of Enterprise*, a bronze water sculpture designed by Tom Lomax. It was intended as a symbolic piece representing Commerce, Industry and Enterprise in the city's past, present and future. Although the sculpture takes prominence in the central grassed area, its dimensions allow it to be understood and appreciated from a pedestrian level. *Forward* was a piece designed by Raymond Mason (1991), in which he used human figures to represent Birmingham's industrial heritage and movement towards industry in the 20th century. Outside Baskerville House sits the *Monument to John Baskerville – Industry and Genius* (1990), in memory of the entrepreneurial printer and originator of the many eponymous typefaces.

These markedly different pieces of public art were very successful in bringing interest and meaning to the square; they came to symbolise both pride in the city's past and its readiness to embrace the future.

A further consideration in the design process was the careful selection of appropriate materials and finishes. The artist Tess Jaray was commissioned to develop designs for the paving, seating, lighting and railings. The paving throughout the square has been arranged using

bricks laid in a mosaic pattern, giving the impression that a large carpet has been laid across the space. The full extent of this can be appreciated from the surrounding buildings, which give striking views into the square.

The civic square was completed in June 1991, when it was formally opened along with the International Convention Centre by Her Majesty the Queen.

Project Sign-off

It is quite clear from the recent history of Centenary Square that the initial brief was indeed successfully implemented; the large numbers of people who daily use the square as a thoroughfare are a testament to the success of this multifunctional space. Since its opening, the square has become the location of the city's New Year's celebrations, in which up to 50,000 people fill the space and spill out onto the adjoining streets. Undoubtedly, the square is a fundamental part of Birmingham's wider strategy of creating an accessible city, connected by a series of streets and public spaces.

Unfortunately, the statue *Forward* by Raymond Mason received mixed opinions and was sadly burnt down during an arson attack in April 2003. In spite of this the remaining pieces of art are much valued, and still considered to be symbolic of the city's historic values and hope for the future.

Collectively, the artworks have certainly provoked great public sentiment and debate within the city. In 1992, the International Convention Centre, Centenary Square, National Indoor Arena and the Repertory Theatre were given the Arts Council / British Gas Cities Award in recognition of the important contribution the arts had made to the regeneration of the city.

In summary, Centenary Square is enjoyed and appreciated as a multifunctional shared space which reflects the past, present and future of this dynamic city.

PROJECT TEAM

Client: **Birmingham City Council**
Architect: **Birmingham Design Services**
Main Contractor: **Impressa Castelli UK Ltd**
Quantity Surveyor: **Birmingham City Council**
Structural Engineer: **Birmingham City Council**
Services Engineer: **Birmingham City Council**
Civil and Drainage Engineer: **Birmingham City Council**
Project Manager: **Birmingham City Council**
Planning Supervisor: **Birmingham City Council**
Lighting Engineer: **Birmingham City Council**
Landscape Architect: **The Landscape Practice Group**
Artists: **Tom Lomax, Tess Jaray and Raymond Mason**

Changing the 'concrete collar', otherwise known as the Inner Ring Road, with the removal of unpleasant and disorientating subways was one of the first steps towards the creation of a more attractive, pedestrian-friendly city-centre environment.

VICTORIA CIVIC SQUARE

THE LANDSCAPE PRACTICE GROUP, BIRMINGHAM CITY COUNCIL

Victoria Square, off Upper New Street and Waterloo Street, Birmingham

Construction Value: £3.7 million
Completion Date: May 1993

Description

A major civic square was created at the heart of the city centre, in place of what had formerly been a very busy traffic junction in front of the Council House. It incorporated a dramatic fountain and a stunning range of sculptural pieces by one of the country's foremost artists.

History

Birmingham's City Centre Strategy was drafted in 1987, and subsequently debated at the City Centre Challenge Symposium held at Highbury Hall in 1988 (thereafter known as the 'Highbury Initiative'). The outcome was a string of major civic-building and public-realm projects over the next 10–15 years, undertaken with the aim of improving the quality of the city-centre environment and attracting new investment – a goal that has been achieved very successfully.

Changing the 'concrete collar', otherwise known as the Inner Ring Road, with the removal of unpleasant and disorientating subways was one of the first steps towards the creation of a more attractive, pedestrian-friendly city-centre environment.

This view was reinforced in the study produced by Don Hilderbrandt of Land Design Research, *Pedestrian Movement and Open Space Strategy*, which advocated an attractive tree-lined-boulevard treatment for the Inner Ring Road, with safer pedestrian crossings linked to a traffic-calmed and pedestrianised city-centre core area. Hilderbrandt proposed connecting everything together with a 'streets-and-squares' philosophy of a network of high-quality urban places and links, and Victoria Square was always considered an important part of that particular initiative.

Client's Brief

- To design and build a new civic square on the site of a traffic junction, using high-quality, long-lasting materials sympathetic to the Council House and other fine historic buildings surrounding the space.

- To exclude all traffic from the area, with the exception of service and emergency vehicles.

- To create a user-friendly pedestrian environment, easily negotiable and accessible to people with disabilities.

- To create a large uninterrupted space in front of the Council House for major civic events, and to create a smaller-scale space in the lower part of the piazza to accommodate more intimate events.

Design Process

The basic design aims were to create a high-quality, durable, low-maintenance civic square of modern character that would relate comfortably to the surrounding Grade I and II listed Victorian buildings. The new piazza was also designed to reflect Birmingham's growing stature as a major and progressive European city.

The design team worked closely with Aston University's Civil Engineering Department to produce a scale model of the proposed fountain in order to test and refine its hydraulic characteristics before construction.

The water feature and planters were clad in hard, fine-grained Derbyshire sandstone extracted from the same quarry that was used for the stone of the Council House. The majority of the paving was designed to take heavy vehicular loading. Buff brindle clay paviors have been used throughout the square, with Yorkstone setts laid to a sunburst pattern emanating from the outer rim of the

115

116

upper pool in the fountain, and slabs to add definition and break down the extensive areas of clay paving.

A fibre-optic lighting system was produced to provide light within and immediately around the fountain, with more conventional free-standing, pole-mounted electric lamps placed at strategic points about the square and supplemented by floodlighting units mounted on the surrounding buildings. The overall type, colour and distribution of light and lighting installations within the square and upon the surrounding buildings was considered holistically from the outset.

A bespoke range of site furniture (railings, seats, litter bins and lamps) was produced for the scheme to reinforce the square's unique character and sense of place.

Large semi-mature trees were planted to add height, maturity and greenery quickly. Bedding displays and hanging baskets on the light columns provide colour all the year round.

The Arts Council were approached to advise on the appointment, by invitation, of a select number of artists who were available to work immediately with the other design-team members, as the project had to be delivered to a very tight timescale.

Dhruva Mistry was subsequently appointed as the principal artist responsible for the range of sculptures produced for Victoria Square — comprising the bronze river goddess and young adults within the fountain, and the stone guardians and obelisk lanterns sited at the top and bottom of the flight of steps around the central fountain.

The Carving Workshop cut the stonework under Mistry's direction. Bettina Furnee was responsible for all of the letter-carving on site, and the cast-iron Christmas tree pit cover.

In addition, the existing statue of Queen Victoria was removed from its pedestal and taken away to be cleaned, re-varnished and reinstalled in good time before the completion of the main contract.

A further statue, the *Iron Man*, produced by Antony Gormley, was commissioned by the TSB bank and sited in front of the former GPO building, overlooking Victoria Square.

Project Sign-off

The objectives of the clients' brief had to be achieved within a very tight timescale (11 months), and with minimum disruption to the city centre — an outcome achieved through careful planning, design and execution.

This former traffic junction has been transformed into a genuine civic square, with some superb public artworks, which Birmingham people have christened fondly with a variety of colloquial names. It is a place where Brummies and visitors alike can sit, meet and take in the sights; a year-round venue for city-centre events; and a fine setting, with the water feature and Council House as backdrop, for many a casual photograph or more formal photocall.

PROJECT TEAM

Client: **Birmingham City Council**

Architect: **The Landscape Practice Group, Birmingham City Council**

Main Contractor: **Impresa Castelli UK Ltd**

Quantity Surveyor: **Corporate Services Department, Birmingham City Council**

Co-ordinating Engineer: **Birmingham City Council**

Structural Engineer: **Birmingham City Council**

Services Engineer: **Birmingham City Council**

Lighting Engineer: **Birmingham City Council**

Hydraulic Engineer: **Civil Engineering Department, Aston University**

Resident Engineer: **City Engineers' Department, BCC**

Project Manager: **Birmingham City Council**

Planning Supervisor: **Birmingham City Council**

Landscape Architect: **The Landscape Practice Group**

Public Art Consultant: **Arts Council**

Principal Artist: **Dhruva Mistry**

Artists: **Jamie Sargeant, Peter Kellock, Richard Holliday, Andy Grey and Bettina Furnee, The Carving Workshop**

The concept for the park is essentially that of a series of interlinked green spaces, strongly defined as a whole through its real or implied thresholds.

EASTSIDE CITY PARK

PATEL TAYLOR ARCHITECTS WITH ALLAIN PROVOST

Eastside, Birmingham

Construction Value: £12 million
Completion Date: 2009

Description

Eastside City Park is a linear park within the regeneration precinct of Birmingham Eastside. It extends eastwards from Park Street, along the frontage of Millennium Point to the Digbeth Branch Canal. It is designed as a series of well-articulated spaces which make topographical, historical and formal connections to the city.

History

The Eastside precinct, which comprises some 170 hectares, is located to the north of historic Digbeth – the birthplace of Birmingham's industrial economy. The eastern boundary of the park is the Digbeth Branch Canal, a significant part of the story of the city's industrial past, which connects to the Birmingham and Fazeley Canal to the north and the Grand Union Canal to the east. To the west of the park is a former burial ground containing archaeological remains, and there are significant historical buildings adjoining the main body of the park, including the former Curzon Street Railway Station.

Client's Brief

The vision for the regeneration of Eastside derives from a thriving creative-industry and digital-media sector, which is supported by the learning and technology activity around the site of the park: Millennium Point combines a science museum with a centre for technological innovation, whilst Aston University and Aston Science Park are established learning centres. The required roles of the park are numerous: firstly, to provide amenity space in a city which is lacking in central green space; secondly, to address the immediate and larger physical context; thirdly, to acknowledge and reinforce the heritage of Birmingham and the specific history of the site; and, finally, to be a place which inspires creativity by virtue of its design and through its capacity to accommodate events – art,

spontaneous activity and social interchange. The client acknowledged that the quality and character of the spaces envisaged are not necessarily reflected in the traditional notions of parkland, so part of the brief was to challenge the accepted idea of 'park'.

Design Process

The concept for the park is essentially that of a series of interlinked green spaces, strongly defined as a whole through its real or implied thresholds. On one level, its linear form lends itself to a continuous narrative from west to east, from informality to formality, from higher to lower ground, from the city centre to the intercity connections. On another level, it aims to be largely 'osmotic' transversely, in that it draws participants to its perimeter, before allowing them to experience the park in various different ways.

The threads which make up the fabric of this concept are as follows:

- The Park is a *room* for the city: the structure of the park implies a virtual room, which is defined through a flexible framework and accommodates the dynamics of the city over time. This room is connected to other developments through formal architectural strategies: viewing corridors, axial pathways and topographical continuity through the remodelling of roads and pavements. The room is also orientated to be parallel to the front elevation of Millennium Point, and as such not only anticipates entry but also provides possibilities for the extension of exhibition spaces laterally. Finally, the room is part of a series of other public spaces embedded in the city – Brindleyplace, Centenary Square, Chamberlain Square, Victoria Square and Cathedral Square.

PATEL TAYLOR

- The Park is *linear*, with three gardens: the Serpentine
  Garden to the west, which makes visible the existing
  archaeological remains; the central Thematic Gardens,
  which comprise an events space with a canopy
  structure followed by three 'character gardens'; and,
  finally, the Water Garden with glasshouse, connecting
  to the canal.

- The Park is a place for both *memory and the creation
  of memories*. Its design engages with the local
  history of the site and the history of the city through
  the implied continuity of water as a theme, from
  the recovery of the historical ditch in the Serpentine
  Garden to the reoccurring weirs leading to the canal.
  Simultaneously, the design exaggerates the level
  change from city centre to canal by sloping each
  garden one level below the perimeter datum of
  Millennium Point: the participant's awareness of the
  existing topography is, therefore, heightened. Finally, it
  is through the richness of each successive garden that
  the park creates various settings for different activities,
  day or night, throughout the year.

- The Park is a place for *joy*. Any great civic space
  creates a unique sense of place and allows activities
  to unfold spontaneously. The articulation of the design
  of the park will undergo further development to ensure
  that this fundamental element of the concept is
  intrinsic.

Project Sign-off

The project is currently at concept design stage, but it
is anticipated that it will progress rapidly after receiving
planning consent.

DAVE BAGNALL/IMAGES OF BIRMINGHAM

PROJECT TEAM

Client: **Birmingham City Council**
Architect: **Patel Taylor Architects with Allain Provost**
Main Contractor: **Not yet appointed**
Quantity Surveyor: **Davis Langdon**
Structural Engineer: **Ove Arup & Partners**
Services Engineer: **Ove Arup & Partners**
Civil Engineer: **Ove Arup & Partners**
Lighting Engineer: **Ove Arup & Partners**
Traffic Engineer: **Ove Arup & Partners**
Sustainability Consultant: **Ove Arup & Partners**
Landscape Architect: **Allain Provost and Parklife**

RETAIL AND COMMERCE

ALL IMAGES ON THIS SPREAD CRAIG HOLMES/IMAGES OF BIRMINGHAM

The projects in this section encompass the best of Birmingham's commercial and retail development over the past decade and a half. With Brindleyplace, Birmingham was fortunate to welcome Argent into the city, one of the most enlightened property developers currently operating in the UK.

With a masterplan initially drawn up by Terry Farrell and later refined by John Chatwin, Brindleyplace has become a benchmark for mixed-use inner-city commercial development. After spearheading the development of Brindleyplace for Argent, Alan Chatham then went on to start his own company, the Mailbox, now followed by the Birmingham Development Company. Chatham, working with Associated Architects, achieved what many thought was impossible, by taking the hulking 1970s former Royal Mail sorting offices and turning them into a mixture of upmarket shopping, restaurants, offices and apartments. The Mailbox not only convinced the BBC to relocate from Pebble Mill, it helped refocus the city back on its hidden waterways, the miles of canal that connect Birmingham's characterful old industrial areas with the rejuvenated city centre. Make's new Cube development will add a further, even more exciting, architectural flourish to the canalside redevelopment begun by Mailbox.

Both these schemes, Brindleyplace and Mailbox, helped create the environment in which outside investors felt confident enough to create the new Bullring shopping centre. Birmingham, so long a backwater in terms of shopping and consumer leisure, has been reinvented over the past 15 years. Once languishing in the lower leagues of British shopping cities, Birmingham is now rated

amongst the very best in the country. This change in fortunes has been almost entirely down to one single development, the Bullring. The Birmingham Alliance's immense retail complex is essentially an out-of-town shopping centre bolted on to the side of the city centre, and although some have criticised the way that it relates to its surroundings it is difficult to ignore the fact that it has changed perceptions of the city for millions of visitors.

During the 1980s, out-of-town shopping centres, such as Merry Hill near Dudley, went from strength to strength. The car- and share-owning democracy which Margaret Thatcher helped to create turned its back on many traditional high streets and instead headed (in its cars) to the massive shopping malls that sprang up from abandoned industrial landscapes all over the United Kingdom. City centres bore the brunt of this exodus of shoppers – with Birmingham losing all but one of its department stores during the decade, leaving behind a barren and depressing city centre. By the early 1990s, the Major government had woken up to the damage that the out-of-town stores were doing, and clamped down on their further expansion – but the question still remained of how centres such as Birmingham could regain their positions as regional shopping destinations. Birmingham's answer was to bring the out-of-town mall back into the city, and that is exactly what was achieved with the Bullring. With around 150 retail outlets and two 'anchor' department stores, the Bullring almost doubled the retail space of the city centre at a stroke. Although immense, it has also successfully reopened historic routes and views from New Street down into Digbeth. And it has, of course, given Birmingham its first truly iconic piece of modern architecture, Future Systems' internationally recognised Selfridges department store.

The design team established the
need for a principal point of focus
at the heart of the space – the
Piers Gough café.

BRINDLEYPLACE PUBLIC REALM –
MAIN SQUARE AND OOZELLS SQUARE
TOWNSHEND LANDSCAPE ARCHITECTS

Brindleyplace, Birmingham

Main Square
Construction Value: £2.5 million   **Completion Date:** 1995

Oozells Square
Construction Value: £800 thousand   **Completion Date:** 1998

Description

A series of new squares and streets, designed to link
Brindleyplace into the surrounding area and to establish
the development as a major destination in its own right.

History

A former industrial site close to the heart of the city's
canal network, Brindleyplace came about as a result
of the city council's decision to build a new convention
centre on adjacent land. The development went through
numerous masterplans and owners, before eventually
being bought by Argent in the early 1990s.

Client's Brief

In 1994, Argent invited Townshend Landscape Architects
to enter a competition to design the main square for their
newly acquired site at Brindleyplace. The competition
brief, which included the initial urban design guidelines
prepared by John Chatwin, called for the square to:

- act as a natural extension to the sequence of public
  spaces running through the centre of Birmingham;

- be of sufficient stature to create an 'address' at the
  heart of the development, whilst also relating to the
  buildings that were going to border it;

- be an integral part of the network of public spaces
  that would link all parts of Brindleyplace, but which at
  that time were loosely defined;

- accommodate all the necessary service and servicing
  routes associated with a development of this size;

- be sufficiently robust to respond to change over time,
  and yet retain its character;

- be capable of being built within the prescribed budget
  and development programme.

To this was added an aspiration to create a dynamic
space, imbued with a spirit of optimism at a time when
the economy was beginning to show signs of recovery.

Design Process

Analysis of the early masterplan established an
understanding of the anticipated vistas, circulation routes,
microclimatic conditions and changes in level. From this,
the design team established the need for a principal point
of focus at the heart of the space – the Piers Gough
café – which would terminate the views into the site
from the International Convention Centre, Broad Street
and Sheepcote Street, and provide a hub of activity and
movement. Secondary points were identified at the ends
of the east–west diagonal axis across the square, which
would strengthen the pedestrian links with the ICC and
terminate one of the principal views across the square.
These points became the water feature to the east, where
the moving water captures and reflects the light throughout
the day, and the Miles Davies sculpture to the west, which
acts as a reminder of the historic past of Brindleyplace.
By utilising the change in level across the site, an
amphitheatre was created in the centre of the square
adjacent to the café – in the warmest and sunniest spot.

The change in level of approximately one metre east
to west across the square allowed the introduction
of a series of strata, each indicating a different use.
At the upper level to the east, the simply patterned
Yorkstone paving addresses the fronts of Buildings Two
and Three, and also accommodates the fire route and
other emergency-services needs. The sinuous limestone
steps double-up as seats as well as forming a cascade,
and cast varying shadows under the changing lighting
conditions. The starburst pattern, made up of only two
differently dimensioned modules of York stone, radiates
from the café, emphasising the active use of the space

as well as reinforcing the focus on the building. The tilting grass planes contain and shield the café from the road on the west side, and provide a pool of colour throughout the year. Finally, the trees – sweetgum (or *Liquidambar styraciflua*) on the south side and *Ginkgo biloba* on the north – anchor the corners of the square.

At night, the square takes on a different character. The fountains become candles; lit from beneath, they entrap the light as they rise and fall in endless variations. The café sheds glowing light through its transparent skin, while the sculpture and trees are more softly uplit to mark the extremities of the space.

Oozells Square was not identified as an open space in the original masterplan. But a review of the plan by the design team, along with a perceived demand for more restaurant and leisure activities grouped around further open space, led to its designation as such. Its brief was similar to that for the main square – except that this was to be a space with a strong individual identity, which would complement and not compete with the main square. This was helped by the presence of the former school, which had become the Ikon Gallery, at the east

end of Oozells Square – and by the strongly linear form of the space itself.

A simple but strong response was required to connect the two ends of the space. To achieve this, a rill of water was positioned to run diagonally across the square, focusing on the tower of the Ikon Gallery at one end and on a tree at the other. This tree was, in turn, positioned to frame the views from Broad Street to the entrance of the proposed Number Seven building. The centre of the square, across which the rill runs before disappearing at either end, was set lower to distinguish it from the surrounding circulation routes, as well as to provide a frame for the sculptor Paul de Monchaux to insert the family of sculptures which he was creating for the space. This area is surfaced with a self-sealing Raisby gravel, giving it a soft finish when kept raked but allowing it to double as a boules allée during the summer months.

The frame around this sunken area, a limestone step, is reinforced by lines of trees. White flowering cherries were chosen for the brilliance of their colour as well as for the carpet of petals they create, marking a simple but strong event in the calendar. At night the trees are

ALL IMAGES ON THIS SPREAD CRAIG HOLMES/IMAGES OF BIRMINGHAM

uplit. This is the only light source in the space other than the rill, which is lit from hidden sources beneath the water at each end. The rill is carved out of blocks of black granite and brings a line of light down to the ground plane. This constantly flowing stream is randomly disturbed by a pulse, creating the illusion of water running uphill.

The pedestrian areas on the upper level are laid in York stone, using pieces of the same dimensions as in the starburst pattern of the main square but in a simple broken bond. Vehicular areas are finished with reclaimed Yorkstone sets retrieved from the remnants of a number of the old roads on the site.

Project Sign-off

The public spaces at Brindleyplace have been widely recognised as integral to its success. Not only do they provide a pleasant refuge for the many people that work within or visit Brindleyplace, but they have raised the standard by which commercial developments are judged elsewhere within the city.

PROJECT TEAM

MAIN SQUARE
Client: **Argent Group plc**
Architect: **Townshend Landscape Architects**
Main Contractor: **Tilbury Douglas**
Employers Agents/ Quantity Surveyor: **Silk and Frazier**
Main contractors design team:
Structural Engineer: **Arup**
Services Engineer: **Arup**
Planning Supervisor: **Silk and Frazier**

OOZELLS SQUARE
Client: **Argent Group plc**
Architect: **Townshend Landscape Architects**
Main Contractor: **Kyle Stewart**
Employers Agents/ Quantity Surveyor: **Silk and Frazier**
Main contractors design team:
Structural Engineer: **Kyle Stewart Design Services**
Services Engineer: **Kyle Stewart Design Services**
Planning Supervisor: **Silk and Frazier**

In response to the vertical scale of the buildings surrounding the square, the single-storey café asserts itself vertically by means of butterfly extensions to the roof.

BRINDLEYPLACE CAFÉ

CZWG ARCHITECTS

The square at Brindleyplace, Birmingham

Construction Value: £380 thousand
Completion Date: May 1997

Description

A free-standing café as a sculptural centrepiece to Brindleyplace square.

History

At the time of CZWG's appointment, the location of a circular café within the development had been determined by the masterplanner and landscape architect. The lozenge-shaped footprint of the resulting design required a small adjustment of the landscape around it.

Client's Brief

The client required a café / bar seating 40 people with kitchen, lavatories, and basement for storage and fountain pumps. Seating for 100 additional covers was to spread out into the main Brindleyplace square.

Design Process

This café, the evolution of a previous design by CZWG for the site, was predicated on the appointment of an operator requiring a bar licence. Its *raison d'être* is a facility that

ALL IMAGES ON THIS SPREAD CRAIG HOLMES/IMAGES OF BIRMINGHAM

opens out and spreads into the square. A long crescent-shaped bar runs the length of the building, and backs onto the kitchen and lavatories. The seating area is surrounded by glazing to give views onto the square.

In response to the vertical scale of the buildings surrounding the square, the single-storey café asserts itself vertically by means of butterfly extensions to the roof. Glazing comprises predominantly double-glazed units with a white-dot-fritted outer pane. The canopy has the same frit but is single glazed, which helps protect against glare and solar gain.

The structure is sculptural, consisting of a tubular steel frame between which are suspended fully glazed panels. Vertical structural columns are contiguous with the roof members, and cross over at the ridge to form canopies which mirror the footprint of the building. The tubes of the frame are all the same diameter, but vary in wall thickness to accommodate their differing spans and cantilevers. Specially extruded aluminium sections were produced to secure the glazing generally, and also to incorporate weather seals around the plate-glass doors. At only 14 m by 7.6 m wide at its broadest point, the café seats 40 people with provision for over 100 alfresco covers.

Project Sign-off

The 'eye-shaped' glass-and-steel building is at the centre of a radial pattern of Yorkstone paving within an intensive landscape of semi-mature trees, sculpture, a large water feature and grassed areas. The café is CZWG's response to the client's requirement for a visual and poetic focal point for the new commercial development at Brindleyplace.

PROJECT TEAM

Client: **Argent Group plc**
Architect: **CZWG Architects**
Main Contractor: **Kyle Stewart**
Steel Frame Contractor: **Littlehampton Welding**

127

The massing of Three Brindleyplace is additive:
it presents a civic front on the side of the
square and steps down to three storeys
towards Birmingham Canal at the rear.

CRAIG HOLMES/IMAGES OF BIRMINGHAM

CRAIG HOLMES/IMAGES OF BIRMINGHAM

CRAIG HOLMES/IMAGES OF BIRMINGHAM

THREE BRINDLEYPLACE

PORPHYRIOS ASSOCIATES

Brindleyplace, Birmingham

Construction Value: £13 million
Completion Date: 1998

Description

Brindleyplace is a masterplanned, mixed-use development with office buildings, shops, restaurants, housing, leisure buildings and with Oozells Street School restored as a gallery. Designed by different architects, the buildings follow the masterplan which produces an urban pattern of streets converging around two public squares and the canal front.

History

Number Three Brindleyplace was one of the first tranche of major office buildings commissioned for the development. Porphyrios Associates were involved from an early stage in developing a common design code that governed the formal composition of each office block and ensured a consistent urban-design approach throughout.

Client's Brief

Argent Group plc required a landmark office block that would act as a signpost for the wider Brindleyplace development. They also required that the building should work within the John Chatwin masterplan, respecting the adjacent structures already completed or under construction.

Design Process

The massing of Three Brindleyplace is additive: it presents a civic front on the side of the square and steps down to three storeys towards Birmingham Canal at the rear. The tower rises as if embedded within the urban block, and serves as a landmark for the entire Brindleyplace development. The main entrance leads through a double-height arcade into a lofty foyer, which in turn opens onto the central seven-storey glazed atrium.

The atrium is the heart of the building, revealing at once its organisation in plan and section. It has an ashlar stone base with an arcade at ground-floor level, a columniated middle, and a crowning loggia surmounted by a glazed roof. The aim here has been to project a light post-and-beam structure in contrast to the solidity of the external masonry, thereby revealing the two constructional principles of load-bearing wall masonry and steel-frame structure at work. At each office level, lifts open onto broad balconies overlooking the atrium. The 13 m deep floorplate and 2.7 m floor-to-ceiling heights provide excellent working conditions, with ample natural light and potential for natural ventilation.

The building has a steel frame with external walls in self-supporting brick and ashlar stone construction. All architectural projections and rusticated surfaces are in reconstituted stone. Windows are detailed in metal, and roofs are in terne-coated steel sheeting. Generally, the elevations are organised into three sections: a rusticated base, a middle and an attic floor. Cornices, window surrounds and string-courses all lend the building a sculptural character, and ornamental profiles underline its constructional 'reading' while motifs such as anthemia, reeds, roundels and acroteria are used as punctuation devices or to soften its skyline.

Along the elevation to the main square, the interweaving of the arcade arches imparts a pictorial depth to the plane of the wall, with half-round relieving arches transferring the weight onto piers and quarter-engaged Doric columns. Thus a figure-ground dialogue emerges: from a structural viewpoint, the half-round arch is the figure, whilst the pointed arch becomes a figure only on account of the resultant void. This constant oscillation in the reading of figure and ground is heightened further by the memory of the trabeated system to which the Doric columns allude. Here, where the building addresses the public square, the history of western structural traditions is narrated in stone.

Project Sign-off

Number Three Brindleyplace is a serious expression of one practice's continuing engagement with a pre-modernist historical tradition, executed with confidence and flair. It succeeds thanks to the sophistication with which the building has been handled, underlining the validity of the pluralistic approach towards architectural style that was adopted within the wider development.

PROJECT TEAM

Client: **Argent Group plc**
Architect: **Porphyrios Associates**
Main Contractor: **HBG Kyle Stewart**
Quantity Surveyor: **Davis Langdon LLP**
Structural Engineer: **Ove Arup and Partners**
Services Engineer: **Ove Arup and Partners**

CRAIG HOLMES/IMAGES OF BIRMINGHAM

CRAIG HOLMES/IMAGES OF BIRMINGHAM

Four Brindleyplace is the largest
building on the main square, and
backs on to the canal.

FOUR BRINDLEYPLACE

STANTON WILLIAMS

Brindleyplace, Birmingham

Construction Value: £15 million
Completion Date: June 1999

Description

A major new energy-efficient office building, developed
as part of a model of urban regeneration. The previously
derelict site was transformed into an award-winning
flexible office space, restaurant and car park for large or
small organisations.

History

Argent Group acquired the Brindleyplace site, the UK's
largest inner-city mixed development plot, with planning
permission for more than 93,000 m^2 of offices, in 1993,
following the collapse of the developer Rosehaugh.

The masterplan, by John Chatwin, encompassed a central
square, offices, housing, bars, restaurants, shops and
cultural buildings including the National Sealife Centre.
Streets, public spaces, paths and bridges are designed
to enhance and sustain activity within the area into the
evenings and weekends, as well as to connect to the
existing city streets.

A variety of architects with a track record of design quality
were chosen for the different buildings, with round-table
design sessions involving the masterplanner, architects
and city planners helping to establish a common approach
to materials, heights, linkages and massing.

Four Brindleyplace is the largest building on the main
square, and backs on to the canal.

Client's Brief

Design quality, flexibility and energy-efficiency were the
key elements of Argent's brief.

While following the masterplan guidelines for footprint,
massing and building lines, the design of each building
was encouraged to evolve as the district took shape.

Four Brindleyplace was a speculative office building which
needed to be able to adapt to organisations of differing
sizes. The total space requirements were for 10,500 m^2 of
offices, 930 m^2 for a restaurant and 127 parking spaces.
To accommodate smaller organisations each floor – of
2,100 m^2 each – needed to be subdividable into four
separate units.

All Brindleyplace buildings were procured on a 'partnering'
basis, involving a design-and-build contractor with their own
team of consultants in addition to the client's architects.
Stanton Williams were commissioned to take the scheme
to detailed design, with a watching brief to the end of
construction to ensure quality was maintained throughout.

Design Process

Stanton Williams won the competition to design Four
Brindleyplace in 1995.

Using sketches and 1:50-scale models to explore the
internal qualities of light and the interplay between solid
and void, the design evolved into a seven-storey building
(with basement parking) with a six-storey foyer with glazed
roof bringing daylight to each floor.

Four Brindleyplace responds in height, materials and
detailing to the adjacent buildings, with a colonnade facing
the square and a restaurant along the eastern part of
its ground floor. Where the building faces the canal and
residential buildings, it steps down and articulates itself
into a series of volumes responding in scale, materials and
fenestration to its immediate surroundings.

The façade steps back at the double-height entrance
area to address the scale of the square, with the external
materials of stone paving and red brickwork being drawn
into the atrium.

In the foyer, two exposed glazed lifts (with a waiting time of less than 30 seconds) bring drama to the space. Movement on the bridges spanning the void brings constant animation to the space. To achieve maximum transparency and openness the circulation core was placed towards the back of the foyer.

The careful application of high-quality materials was key to the philosophy of the building. A bright reflective façade of clear glass was used to draw light into its interior, together with brick to complement surrounding buildings. A matt but warm red Belgian brick was chosen, but treated differently to that on neighbouring structures. Rather than a standard envelope with punched windows, the solidity of the brick was here handled as a mass, with openings carved out. The brickwork is flush-jointed, allowing the masonry to be read as a continuous mass rather than as individual modules – an approach developed through numerous studies considering ways to draw the materials together.

The floorplates can adapt to both cellular and open-plan office layouts. With totally different aspects, each of the four possible discrete offices on each floor has its own character.

Air is force-circulated through every floor to take advantage of the mass of the concrete structure, and occupants can choose their own method of additional environmental controls. There is the potential for either natural displacement ventilation or chilled beams with exposed concrete ceilings which act as a heat sink, opening windows for all perimeter offices, and conventional fan-coil units. These energy-saving advances, together with a comprehensive BMS-monitoring energy system and intelligent lighting that illuminates the path of movement, ensured the building achieved a BREEAM rating of 'Very Good'.

Project Sign-off

The architects' aim was to create a calm, rigorous, logically constructed space for a range of tenants, to be flexible rather than constraining.

Contributing to the regeneration of one of the UK's great cities, the quality of the design, materials and construction was paramount – a philosophy embraced by the developer Argent, and by those chosen to be part of the area's renewal.

Architecture Today commented that the building 'remains a model of how everyday building can become extraordinary' and Secretary of State for Construction, Nick Raynsford, called it 'the best building of the decade'. It won the Built in Quality Award and the British Council for Offices Regional, National and 'Best of Best' Awards.

PROJECT TEAM

Client: **Argent Group plc**
Architect: **Stanton Williams**
Main Contractor (Design-and-Build Contractor): **Carillion**
Quantity Surveyor: **Silk & Frazier**
Structural Engineer: **Curtins**
Services Engineer: **Hoare Lea & Partners**
Project Manager: **Argent Group Plc**
Fire Engineer: **Ove Arup & Partners**

131

The client required maximum exploitation of the extremely restricted site to provide well-designed open-plan, Grade 'A' floorplates able to be subdivided into separate tenancies.

ELEVEN BRINDLEYPLACE

GLENN HOWELLS ARCHITECTS

Brindleyplace, Birmingham

Construction Value: £19 million
Completion Date: January 2009

Description

Eleven Brindleyplace will be a landmark building, located at an important gateway to the Brindleyplace estate.

The 15-storey, new-build development will comprise a ground-floor retail / restaurant unit of approximately 300 m², plus 10,000 m² of high-quality Grade 'A' commercial office space.

History

Brindleyplace, with its rich mix of offices and amenities, has become a new focus of Birmingham city life. The provision of a major public open space – as well as retail, leisure, cultural and residential buildings – was a fundamental part of creating a new quarter which would continue to be active into the evenings and at weekends.

The masterplan also aimed to provide an urban framework for a set of buildings, each designed by leading architects, that are related to each other and to their larger context but which combine to create a sense of place and clear identity for Brindleyplace.

Masterplanning guidelines covered strategic matters such as massing and the selection of materials: most buildings share a tripartite elevational treatment with a base (street-level arcade), middle (repetitive office floorplates) and an articulated top. No attempt was made to dictate stylistic uniformity – indeed, the chosen architects represent a diverse range of styles.

Glenn Howells Architects were commissioned in July 2005 to develop proposals for Eleven Brindleyplace, the final phase of development on the estate.

Client's Brief

Intensive feasibility investigations explored numerous options for the site including mixed-use, residential and commercial uses. Research into the Birmingham office market identified a significant demand for high-quality office space at this prime location in the city.

The client required maximum exploitation of the extremely restricted site to provide well-designed open-plan, Grade 'A' floorplates able to be subdivided into separate tenancies. This would offer the flexibility to respond to different market conditions, and create competition as an alternative to the predominantly very large or refurbished office spaces available in the city.

Changing attitudes, both politically and from the marketplace, regarding sustainability issues such as global warming, resource depletion and pollution have influenced the client's decision to demand the first BREEAM 'Excellent' rated new-build office scheme in Birmingham city centre.

Design Process

The design approach acknowledges principles set out in the masterplan in order to provide a framework that follows a clear set of rules in defining the top, middle and bottom of each individual building. However, it also responds to the flexibility and freedom afforded to individual designers to add a new dynamic layer to the estate. The aim with this particular project is to deliver a landmark building and an appropriate gateway element to the western approach of Brindleyplace.

The urban design strategy follows the intentions of the Brindleyplace masterplan in improving the pedestrian thoroughfare through the site and enhancing the public realm. It does this by defining the edges of Brunswick

133

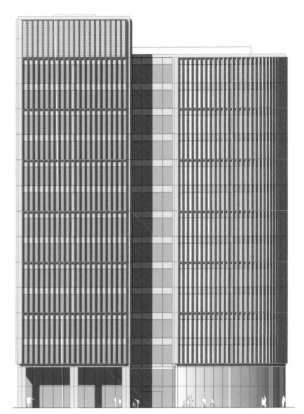

ALL IMAGES ON THIS SPREAD GLENN HOWELLS ARCHITECTS

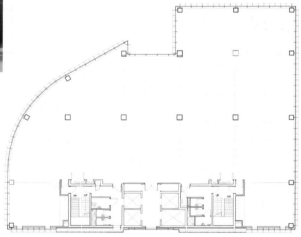

Square and improving the quality of the landscaping. The massing and form respond to their immediate location as well as their placement in the wider context of Brindleyplace and the city. The building form is conceived through distinct elements that address environmental, functional and urban-design issues.

The curved, 13-storey 'shoulder' element provides an appropriate sense of scale for its location at the gateway to the western approach to Brindleyplace. The proximity of this form to the City Inn Hotel further reinforces the sense of arrival to Brindleyplace and closes the corner of Brunswick Square. The rectilinear, 15-storey 'tower' element defines the southwest edge of Brunswick Square and forms the highest point in a cluster of

buildings. It thus provides a visual marker to the west of the estate, reinforcing the dialogue with Number Three to the east. The 'tower' is located between Broad Street and the Brindleyplace car park, and will create dramatic views along this axis. A glazed slot, designed to break up the mass of the building and to define the entrance and lift core, separates the two main elements.

Commercial A1–A3 units are situated at ground-floor level, with full-height glazing to activate the frontage. The colonnade in front of the 'tower' provides a sense of enclosure and a further layering to the ground-floor façade. Visitors are drawn towards the entrance, which is expressed through the glazed slot between the two distinct building elements. The dramatic height of the lobby space, transparent façade and continuity of architectural language between inside and outside imply an extension of the public realm into the building.

The building has been arranged around a single core to maximise the efficiency of the floorplates. The position of this core also overcomes some potentially difficult environmental and legislative factors whilst also informing the expression of the important rear elevation. It is located along the southwest façade to limit the amount of office space exposed to solar gain.

The façade design follows the masterplanning guidelines for Brindleyplace, which require a tripartite elevational treatment with a base (street-level arcade), middle (office floorplates) and top. The elevation also reinforces the massing strategy by responding to functional, environmental and urban-design issues. The base of the building, enclosing active ground-floor spaces, is enveloped by a curtain-wall system comprising a bronze anodised aluminium frame and high-performance glass that doesn't compromise on transparency. This treatment is also used to express the lightness of the entrance and lift-core slots. Textured, stone-effect panels impart a robustness to the base of the building and establish a dialogue with the predominantly stone and masonry buildings situated within Brindleyplace. The material is also utilised as a full-height rain-screen cladding system on the rear elevation adjacent to the Novotel service yard.

Office floors also benefit from floor-to-ceiling clear glazed curtain-walling, with insulated enamel-faced glass spandrel units masking the floor structure. An additional layering is added to the façade through the use of 300 mm deep by 70 mm wide bronze anodised-aluminium vertical 'baguettes' attached to the outside of the curtain-wall at regular pitches around the building. These create an expressive play of depth and texture on the façade, but also prevent excessive solar gains and help reduce annual building energy use and carbon emissions – particularly at the corners of the building, where glazing is located on two different orientations and high solar gains are likely to occur. The vertical shading also helps to maximise daylight into the office space, which would otherwise have had to be reduced by alternative horizontal shading systems.

The core at the rear of the building is expressed as a solid element utilising glass-reinforced concrete rain-screen panels with feature anodised-aluminium inset profiles, which continue the 'language' of the office façades and break up the mass of the elevation facing Broad Street.

The colours and finishes chosen for the anodised-aluminium and glass-reinforced concrete convey warmth and respond to their local context within Brindleyplace.

The 'crown' of the building, screening plant on levels 13 and 14, is an important element of the development. The top of the building is visible from many points around the city and, therefore, needed to be expressed as a strong, confident form by day and night. It is proposed that a light-box feature is installed – one which uses a reflective, fritted glass screen, modulated with a profiled bronze anodised-aluminium shadow detail, to continue the language created by the *brise-soleil* treatment on the main façade below.

Project Sign-off

The key objective throughout the project has been to build and continue Argent's reputation for delivering high-quality, design-led developments. This has been realised through working creatively and in close collaboration with the client and the design team to produce an elegant and highly functional building on a difficult site and under a strict budget.

Eleven Brindleyplace will be a landmark building, forming the final piece in Argent Estates' Brindleyplace development which has, to great acclaim, successfully extended the city centre of Birmingham westwards.

Work is now well underway on Eleven Brindleyplace, with completion due early in 2009.

PROJECT TEAM

Client: **Argent Group PLC**
Architect: **Glenn Howells Architects**
Main Contractor: **HBG Construction**
Quantity Surveyor : **Faithful+Gould**
Structural Engineer: **HBG Design**
Services Engineer (Concept): **Ove Arup & Partners**
Services Engineer (Detailed): **HBG Design**
Project Manager: **Faithful+Gould**
CDM Coordinator: **Faithful+Gould**
Fire Consultant: **Faber Maunsell**

The client required an outdoor
space that would act as a focus
for special events within the
redeveloped Bullring.

ST MARTIN'S SQUARE, CENTRAL STREET AND ROTUNDA SQUARE

GROSS MAX

St Martin's Square, Bullring, Birmingham

Completion Date: September 2003

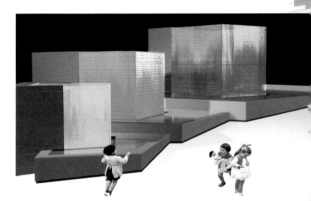

Description

A new public space at the heart of the redeveloped
Bullring shopping centre, creating a context for the
historic St Martin's Church and the dramatic new
Selfridges store by Future Systems.

History

The site had been the historic heart of medieval
Birmingham, around the parish church of St Martins. The
old Bull Ring had been a steeply inclined street leading
up from Digbeth to the bottom of New Street and High
Street. It was the historic location of the city's cattle
market, and the home of the almost 1,000-year-old
outdoor retail markets. During the Second World War
the area experienced some bomb damage, and then in
the early 1960s the creation of the new Inner Ring Road
and new Bullring shopping centre saw the entire area
completely demolished. The resulting redevelopment was
initially hailed as a revolutionary step forward but over
time came to be seen as a catastrophic mistake, cutting
off Digbeth from the rest of the city and destroying a
much-loved and unique part of the city's historic core.
The Birmingham Alliance's total redevelopment of the
shopping centre allowed some of these past mistakes
to be corrected, with surface-level pedestrian movement
restored across the site and a new large open space
created around the church.

MICHAEL BETTS

Client's Brief

The client required an outdoor space that would act as a
focus for special events within the redeveloped Bullring.
It was also seen as desirable to create an attractive
and high-quality space in which shoppers would feel
comfortable, and from which they would be able to
appreciate the surrounding buildings.

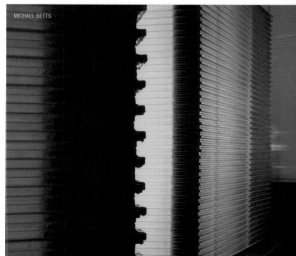

MICHAEL BETTS

136

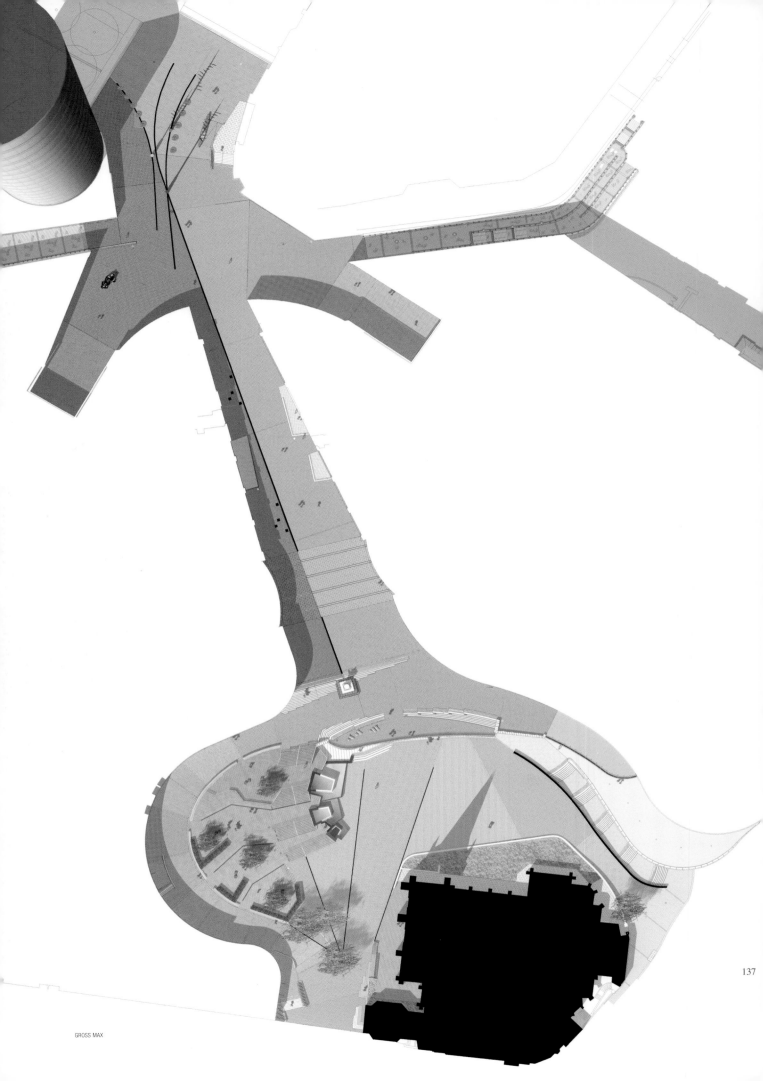

GROSS MAX

CRAIG HOLMES/IMAGES OF BIRMINGHAM   PAUL WARD/IMAGES OF BIRMINGHAM

Design Process

The new Bullring, which replaces a 1960s development, takes advantage of a natural slope by creating streets and open spaces on different levels. The development is the latest addition in a sequence of public spaces which have been newly created as part of Birmingham's inner-city regeneration. The architecture of the commercial buildings is a mixture of the ordinary and the sublime, with the new Selfridges store by Future Systems as iconic landmark. The 'Yves Klein blue' façade of this striking department store is clad with 15,000 anodised aluminium discs, inspired by the chain-mail dress designs of Paco Rabanne. The effect of the changing sky reflected on the curved building's outer skin is extraordinary. Opposite, and in sharp contrast, is the historic landmark of St Martin's Church, which has gained a new and more prominent position at the bottom of a sloping square.

The character of St Martin's Square is determined by its dramatic topography, the prominent position of St Martin's Church and the curvilinear building façade of the Bullring shopping centre. A dramatic combination of cascading water-walls, reflecting pools, steps, terraces and trees negotiate the approximately 8 m level difference. The water feature forms a counterpoint to the new Selfridges building. Illuminated in slow-changing hues of pink, yellow and blue, the water sculpture also provides a visual spectacle for the cafés around the square – acting as a visual break between the limestone terrace areas to the east and the sloping herringbone-granite-paved square to the west. Water cascades down the sides of three glass cubes, ranging from 2, 3 to 5 m in height – each containing a different-coloured 6 mm thick Perspex light box surrounded by 300 mm deep glass walls constructed out of 19 mm thick plates of stacked white glass with clear silicon fixings. Glass columns and beams provide structural support for the walls and 19 mm glass-plate roof. The water flows into a series of slate-clad pools at the base of each cube and is continually recycled and released through a concealed tank. The sequence of different terraces as part of the cascading ensemble of steps and level areas allows for flexible and informal use, while the overall configuration can also be utilised as an amphitheatre for occasional larger-scale events and performances.

Central Street, in between St Martin's Square and Rotunda Square, is paved in two contrasting granites. The street is lit by catenary lighting, allowing ample space for pedestrian circulation and an uninterrupted view towards St Martin's Church spire and a repositioned bronze statue of Nelson

dating from 1809. A terrace with elongated seats forms a viewing platform over the new St Martin's Square and the Church.

Rotunda Square, at the top of Central Street, is strategically located at a crossroads of routes. This position is celebrated by a dramatic sculptural landmark designed by artist Peter Fink of Art 2 Architecture and based on Gross Max's concept of marking the square with three gently swaying 'light wands' which match the height of St Martin's Church spire. The light wands take the form of three coloured carbon-fibre masts rising 20, 25 and 30 m in height. The technology employed is derived from high-performance yacht manufacturing, to provide very strong, yet lightweight structures capable of high wind resistance. The wands feature rotating 'leaves' of stainless steel, which limit the degree of movement in the upper parts of the mast to a gentle swaying. Internally lit, the wands echo the lighting theme used in the water sculpture at St Martin's Square in order to animate the structure at night.

Project Sign-off

The new square has created a high-quality and distinctive new space right at the heart of the city, and also helped restore the visual and pedestrian connections between New Street and Digbeth. From being a barrier to movement and a place to be avoided, the Bullring and St Martin's Square are now key stopping-off points and destinations in their own right.

PROJECT TEAM

Client: **The Birmingham Alliance**
Architect: **Gross Max**
Structural Engineer (water feature): **Dewhurst McFarlane (London)**
Structural Engineer (light wands): **Technica (London)**
Artist (light wands): **Peter Fink, Art 2 Architecture (London)**
Lighting design: **DPA (Edinburgh)**

The site for the café forms a link from the pedestrian ramp, which curves around its western side, to the uppermost terrace itself.

SPIRAL CAFÉ

MARKS BARFIELD ARCHITECTS

Unit 3a, Bullring Shopping Centre, Birmingham

Construction Value: £650 thousand
Completion Date: October 2004

Description

Located in St Martin's Square, the new public space and centrepiece of Birmingham's revitalised Bullring development, the Spiral Café is a distinctive shell-like enclosure inspired by the Fibonacci principles of growth in Nature.

History

The Spiral Café is located on the uppermost of four landscaped terraces on the west side of the plaza surrounding St Martin's Church – the main area of open outdoor space within the Bullring redevelopment. These terraces are formed from 'giant steps' cascading southward to create open pockets of informal seating and recreational space. As such, the café incorporates seasonal exterior covers on the terraces beneath, and in the plaza as a whole.

This plaza is surrounded by several key elements in the Bullring scheme: St Martin's Church – a local landmark Victorian neo-Gothic building, around which the plaza is formed; the main pedestrian thoroughfare through the Bullring; and the new Selfridges department store. To the east of the site, at the focal centre of the square, is a substantial landscaped water feature, consisting of three large glass blocks backlit with coloured light and set into several pools.

The site for the café forms a link from the pedestrian ramp, which curves around its western side, to the uppermost terrace itself. It has a prime aspect to the church and to Selfridges, as well as the terraces below, whilst also being prominently visible from all levels of the surrounding retail development.

Client's Brief

The purpose of this café was to create a landmark structure, which would be part-sculpture and part-revenue-generator, while at the same time helping to animate the terraces of the hard landscaping in which it sits. A high degree of transparency was required to preserve the quality of the landscaping and the illuminated glass water sculpture to the east, and to avoid blocking sight lines to adjacent retail units.

Design Process

With a site sitting at a point between the commerciality of the main scheme and the spirituality of the renovated and striking St Martin's Church, Marks Barfield Architects felt that using a natural geometric order, which was neither spiritual nor commercial, would be an appropriate response to the brief.

The building form is generated according to the universal patterns of growth found within Nature. A Fibonacci spiral has been extruded along a tilting axis to form a simple spiral tunnel, reminiscent of a shell or the double-helix shape found in sunflower-seed heads, pine cones or pineapples.

The building is an inviting tunnel, at the threshold of the pedestrian ramp which forms a gateway to the uppermost terrace of the square. Passing through the building, the glazing opens up to reveal the terraces below. The tip of the kiosk's leading edge is aligned with the spire of St Martin's Church opposite.

A series of eight ribs supports the roof, along with 13 perpendicular strips of structure visible from beneath. The spiral form, which creates the roof, is continued under the building and emerges to divide the servery area from the customer space within.

The exterior of the kiosk is rugged and durable, whereas the inside is smooth and precious. The superstructure of

the café comprises painted plasma-cut mild-steel plate connected by circular hollow mild-steel sections for lateral support. This is 'skinned' with a plywood timber decking using a warm-roof construction, and clad externally with post-patinated copper on continuous hermetic self-adhesive WPM. Internally, lacquer-finished bronze panels clad the areas between the ribs, with a stainless-steel capping piece running along each rib-line.

Like a shell, the internal surface of the café forms a 'precious' and warm enclosure. The eight structural ribs are visible through the ceiling; these are in brushed stainless steel to reflect the light. Along the internal curvature of each rib a strip of light picks out its shape, wrapping around the building. Uplighting to this internal face gives general ambient lighting to the café.

From the outside, the building sits like a sculpture, or a beached seashell, sunk slightly into the surrounding landscape. Inside, the space feels open and enchanting, with wide views onto the terraces and the surrounding buildings.

Project Sign-off

The Spiral Café has added life and activity to a new public space, and has been received with delight not only by visitors but also by architectural juries. Awards for the Spiral Café include the BDI Places & Genius Award and the Copper and Architecture in 2005, and an RIBA Award in 2006.

Since opening, the café has been so successful that it has won an international Costa award. They attribute this success in large part to the quality of the architecture, as the café attracts many people who have come to look at the building and then decide to have a cup of coffee.

PROJECT TEAM

Client: **The Birmingham Alliance**
Architect: **Marks Barfield Architects**
Main Contractor: **Thomas Vale**
Quantity Surveyor: **GTCS Gardiner and Theobald**
Structural Engineer: **Price and Myers 3D Engineering**
Services Engineer: **WSP**
Project Manager: **GTMS Gardiner and Theobald**
Planning Supervisor: **GTPS Gardiner and Theobald**
Civil Engineer: **Waterman Engineers**

> The client's brief was to create an inspirational shop that pushed the evolution of their existing retail environments a step further.

KAREN MILLEN – BULLRING

BRINKWORTH

Upper Mall East, Bullring, Birmingham

Completion Date: October 2003

Description

Karen Millen's second UK flagship store. It features a double-height storefront with a huge-scale, brightly coloured titanium-clad 'jewel' feature, in the form of a twisted orthogonal 'box' which punches out into the mall beyond other shopfronts at the store's upper level.

History

Brinkworth have been designing Karen Millen stores for the past 14 years, counting just under 150 outlets worldwide, with each one individually designed and differentiated beyond certain signature elements – in opposition to the mass roll-out design policy of other high-street retailers.

The shop in the Bullring is the second UK flagship store for the brand – alongside the multi-award-winning shop on London's Brompton Road.

Client's Brief

The client's brief was to create an inspirational shop that pushed the evolution of their existing retail environments a step further. Imperative to the project was the idea that the space functioned on an aesthetic as well as a commercial level.

Design Process

For the Bullring store, located on the top level of the mall, Brinkworth responded strongly to The Birmingham Alliance's very open and positive attitude towards innovative retail concepts, creating a piece of landmark architecture within the confines of a shopping-centre context. 'We sketched up a number of real "top-of-the-head" ideas,' said Brinkworth director Adam Brinkworth, 'but the one that stuck was the idea of creating a multi-faceted jewel, set within a non-precious box – inspired by the jewellery of Ben Day, where unmounted stones are cut with all sorts of different facets and faces.'

Underlining the sense of the 'box' as an independent element, the first floor floats free of the shell at the left-hand side and also gives the illusion of floating to the right. The grand-scale (4.5 m high by 1.6 m wide) ground-floor entrance to the store is also set back from the normal mall shopfront lines, exaggerating this first-floor protrusion which also has a strong 'glimpsed' presence throughout the Bullring's circulation atria.

Strong angled lines make up the entire structure, with the ground-floor window splayed slightly to the right to offset the left-angled first-floor 'jewel'. The concrete core of the store is set in maximum contrast to the jewel box above. All other design treatments throughout the premises echo these two contrasts, by either falling into the raw-and-honest materials category that sits with the concrete – or else the highly dramatic and light-reflecting glamour of the titanium box. The ground floor, for example, has a concrete screed floor, wax-buffed but kept raw. Internally lit glass-fibre shelving is not painted out, and shows the quality of the fibreglass. These elements contrast completely with the double-height back wall of the store, made of bevelled and angled 'Vegas' glass. The wall is truly huge-scale, running up through the already-generous 4.5 m ceiling height at ground-floor level to form the whole of the first-floor back wall. The 'Vegas' glass extends to the right-hand wall of the upper-floor space, where it eventually becomes two separate panels following the internal 'crease' of the 'jewel-box' and meeting in an apex.

The half-landing of the staircase offers a great view back into the huge void between the 'jewel box' and the concrete shell. The 5 m high stair is stainless steel with floating metal 'tray' treads, inset with white terrazzo, leading the customer up into the 'belly' of the jewel-box.

On the first floor, the front of the box has an inset window running along the front and wrapping round both its sides.

Like a viewing gallery, this allows views over the mall from its privileged protruding position.

Project Sign-off

Whilst the Brinkworth design team has created a string of strongly individual Karen Millen environments over the past decade and a half, their Bullring store sets itself apart from the rest by being the most eye-catching and dramatic, while still complementing the brand perfectly.

Within the Bullring, where most retailers have made a special effort to capture customers' attention, the jewel-like floating box, matched with the double-height twisted storefront, shows evidence of a confident client who knows their brand and the importance of keeping their customers entertained.

ALL IMAGES ON THIS SPREAD LOUISE MELCHIOR AND LARA GOSLING

PROJECT TEAM

Client: **Karen Millen**
Architect: **Brinkworth**
Main Contractor: **Brian Hart Shopfitting**
Structural Engineer: **Michael Baigent Orla Kelly**
Services Engineer: **Delta Environmental**
Project Manager: **Karen Millen**
Planning Supervisor: **Retailer Made**
Building Control: **National House-Building Council (NHBC)**
Glass work: **Glass Design**

From the outset, this scheme had great ambition. Selfridges required a state-of-the-art department store.

SELFRIDGES

FUTURE SYSTEMS

Upper Mall East, Bullring, Birmingham

Construction Value: £60 million
Completion Date: September 2003

Description

One of two 'anchor' department stores in the new Bullring shopping centre development.

History

Future Systems were appointed by Selfridges' then chief executive, Vittorio Radice, to design only the third store outside of London upon the basis of their previous groundbreaking retail work for Comme Des GarÇons in New York, Tokyo and Paris.

Client's Brief

From the outset, this scheme had great ambition. Selfridges required a state-of-the-art department store. They also wished to have a building that would provide an architectural landmark for Birmingham and an instantly recognisable signpost for the brand. Although Selfridges is physically integrated into the rest of the Bullring, the client wanted a distinct design approach that would set the store apart from the rest of the development. It is this ambition that has driven Future Systems' design.

Design Process

St Martin's Church stands as a landmark of the 19th century; the new Selfridges building is an icon of the 21st century. The relationship between the department store and the church is critical to the development as a whole. Two very different buildings housing two very different functions, they needed to coexist in harmony in order for the wider Bullring redevelopment to succeed. Future Systems sought to create this harmony not from sameness but from contrasts: in form, materials, mood and colour – with each building true to itself, its function and its century.

In response to the natural curve of the site the façade of the Selfridges building is soft and curvaceous, wrapping around the Moor Street / Park Street corner and

ALL IMAGES ON THIS SPREAD CRAIG HOLMES/IMAGES OF BIRMINGHAM

sweeping up to form the roof. In the same way in which the church is truly expressive of its function, Selfridges too, expresses what it is, in a way that is aesthetically innovative but also clearly signifies its function as a department store without the need for signage. This expressive form creates a gentle backdrop to St Martin's, and defines the boundary to the new urban plaza.

The façade of the building is seen as a skin rather than as a conventional cladding system. The unique skin uses conventional rain-screen techniques; innovation comes through the aesthetic, not the technology. A series of anodised aluminium discs clads the building, allowing a loose fit for tolerances and wrapping easily over the double-curved surfaces. Large abstract glazed areas, for shop windows and views in and out from restaurants and offices, are carved out of the overall form.

The department store can be accessed from four entrances: from the shopping mall; the raised terrace facing onto St Martin's Church; the corner of Moor Street and Park Street; and from the bridge link to the car park. A dramatic roof terrace with a high-quality restaurant is open in the evenings as well as during the day.

The ambition for the interior is to match the expectation of the exterior, balancing the curiosity created by the unique façade. The fluidity of the form of the building is matched inside with an organically shaped atrium stretching across the floor plan. This spacious atrium is like an urban canyon, providing shafts of natural light which penetrate deep inside the interior.

Project Sign-off

Selfridges' vision has enabled their store to become a genuine catalyst for urban regeneration in Birmingham. The new Selfridges, together with the shopping mall, have done much to revitalise the Bullring and also point the way for the future development of the Digbeth area.

The building itself has become an instant icon, not only representing the store's brand, but standing for the regeneration and reinvention of Birmingham itself. Not since the Rotunda was built in the 1960s has the city had a building that says quite so clearly, 'This is Birmingham!'

PROJECT TEAM

Client: **Selfridges & Co.**
Architect: **Future Systems**
Main Contractor: **Laing O'Rourke**
Quantity Surveyor: **Boyden & Co.**
Structure Engineer: **Ove Arup & Partners**
Services Engineer: **Ove Arup & Partners**
Project Manager: **Hanscomb**

The building has a confident
modern identity whilst being
sensitive and responsive to its
Conservation Area context.

19 GEORGE ROAD

3DReid

19 George Road, Edgbaston, Birmingham

Construction Value: £2.2 million
Completion Date: January 2007

Description

19 George Road, Edgbaston is Birmingham's first
commercial building ever to receive the BREEAM
(Building Research Establishment's Environmental
Assessment Method) 'Excellent' rating. This 12,545 sq
ft contemporary office space incorporates the latest
requirements for a sustainable building as well as high
levels of insulation and natural day lighting.

History

The site was previously home to a 3 storey office
block known as George House. Built in the 1950's,
it was occupied by the Financial Times until they
relocated out of the area. Calthorpe Estates decided to
demolish this building, which took place in 2002, and
commence a speculative new build office development
in order to improve the quality of the accommodation
and meet the needs of today's occupiers. During the
development process, Calthorpe Estates pre-let the
office accommodation to Shaws, the largest independent
firm of dedicated chartered tax advisers in the UK.

Client's Brief

From the outset there was a specific requirement to
target a BREEAM rating of 'Excellent'. In addition,
the requirement was to achieve as high a density as
possible, whilst maintaining the build costs within a
prescribed limit. The tenant required a design that both
enhanced their public profile from the street, while
also preserving their privacy in what, architecturally, is
otherwise a very traditional street in the leafy suburb of
Edgbaston.

Design Process

The development is based on the concept of a 'floating'
volume set in a green landscaped clearing. To give both

ED MOSS

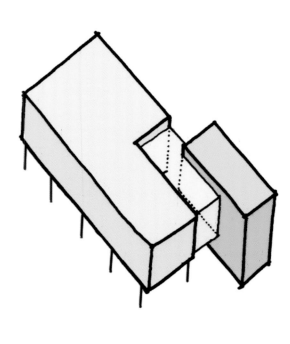

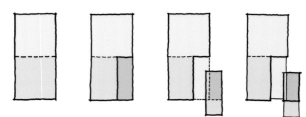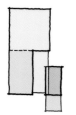

JOHN JAMES

a focus to the scheme and a positive 'aspect' from the internal office environment, a generous internal courtyard has been created affording views into and beyond the space to take advantage of the Conservation Area setting. The plan defines two kinds of office space for 'public and private' accommodation and also a 'core' element containing circulation, reception and services. The core has been pulled away from the main office elements to create the semi-public courtyard space and a meeting and 'break out' space for the tenant.

Energy efficiency has been key to the project's design. A sophisticated digital control system was used to maintain heating, ventilating and cooling systems, which aids in the conservation of energy. High efficiency lamps have been used throughout the building with movement detection, while water consumption is strictly controlled by flow regulators which come with a leak detection system.

Project Sign-off

The building has a confident modern identity whilst being sensitive and responsive to its Conservation Area context. The design also clearly defines and reinforces public and private spaces, while also responding to key environmental and sustainability issues. Absolutely key to the building are its 'green' credentials - 19 George Road has seen Calthorpe Estates set the benchmark for sustainable developments within the West Midlands by achieving Birmingham's first ever BREEAM Offices 'Excellent' rating.

In addition, the development has been awarded three different accolades* for its exceptional environmental and design features. Regional Judges for the British Council for Offices 2007 Awards commented, "This relatively

small, stand-alone office building near the city centre fits well within its surroundings despite the variation in style from its neighbours. The scheme provides an exceptional public profile from the street and has created a strongly structured, finely stylised end product."

In 2007 it was awarded the British Council for Offices 'Small Projects' category award for the Midlands and East Anglia; the 'Sustainable Development of the Year' award at the West Midlands Insider Property Awards; and the 'Green Design' accolade at the Business Design Innovation Awards.

PROJECT TEAM

Client: **Calthorpe Estates**
Architect: **3DReid**
Quantity Surveyor: **DBK Back Ltd**
Structural Engineer: **Waterman Structures**
Services Engineer: **ESC Ltd**
Main Contractor: **Costain Ltd**

151

The old 1960s-built Bullring had become a 'no-go' area for many of Birmingham's residents. Within its low, dark underpasses it had become detached from the heart of the city.

BIRMINGHAM BULLRING

BENOY LTD

Bullring, Birmingham

Construction Value: £280 million
Completion Date: September 2003

Description

The Bullring represents the first of a new generation of inner-city retail developments – comprising over 93,000 m² of retail space within the heart of Birmingham city centre.

History

The old 1960s-built Bullring had become a 'no-go' area for many of Birmingham's residents. Within its low, dark underpasses it had become detached from the heart of the city and, together with the infamous 'Spaghetti junction', stigmatised Birmingham rather like the Gorbals stigmatised Glasgow in the 1950s and 60s.

Client's Brief

The Birmingham Alliance tasked Benoy to reverse the whole 'no-go' tendency of the 1960s Bullring, to open it up and reconnect it to Birmingham's retail quarter so that it would recapture its previous status as the retail heart of the city centre. Furthermore, the client wanted to continue and progress Birmingham's city-centre renaissance by creating generous public spaces: pedestrianised streets and squares which would link and connect to the wider pattern of new public spaces evolving across Birmingham.

Design Process

As the centre of the Midlands' manufacturing base, Birmingham had come to be known as 'motor city'. This idea of Birmingham being car-dominated was further reinforced by its road network, which 'strangled and detached' many parts of the old city; the so-called 'Northern Arm', a major arterial road, severed the old Bullring from the centre of the city.

The first task the architects faced was to reverse this process by completely bridging over the Northern Arm of the Ring Road, allowing the city-centre retail pattern to sweep down

from High Street and New Street to 'seamlessly' connect with the new Bullring. This connection culminates in the new St Martin's Square, giving St Martin's Church – historically the church of Birmingham's markets – its rightful setting in the centre of this new public space.

By treating the entire Bullring area as a city quarter and not a single stand-alone building site, the scale and grain of the surrounding city blocks could be extended into it. Conversely, by breaking the Bullring into similar divisible parts, the various access and connection points around the site could feed directly into the area as a continuation of the existing street patterns and squares.

The direct connection of New Street and High Street, as a continuous 24-hour pedestrianised public street running north–south down to St Martin's Church, divides the site initially into two. It is further divided by the east–west route through and around the Bullring, which links New Street Station on its western edge with Moor Street Station on its eastern side in an additional pedestrianised public route.

Within the Bullring itself, two new department stores form the 'anchors' on its east and west flanks – being further connected by this continuing pattern of internal streets. These internal streets are fully glazed over, their 'skyplane' a 100-per-cent glazed roof structure that allows maximum daylight to percolate down through all three trading levels.

The new Bullring site falls at a gradient of approximately 1 in 12 from its northern to its southern edge. This allowed the architects to build into its slope over 93,000 m² of retail space on three levels.

Active frontage has been incorporated on all of its public faces, to create a feeling of security and well-being at all hours of the day and night.

A rich palette of materials – including natural stone, glass, timber and brickwork – has been used to create a contemporary design which, whilst respecting the nature of the surrounding fabric, takes the Bullring forward into the 21st century as part of a truly European city.

Public spaces within the design have been generously landscaped, and include major public art works – the bronze bull, the kinectic light wands and the illuminated St Martin's Square water feature among them.

Complex car-parking and servicing arrangements have been further incorporated into the sloped site, allowing the built form and public spaces to 'read' clearly without being overpowered by the more functional aspects of the design.

Project Sign-off

Since its opening, the Bullring has been a roaring success – in both commercial and civic terms. It has exceeded all its projected targets and achieved almost 100 per cent letting since day one.

PROJECT TEAM

Client: **The Birmingham Alliance**
Architect: **Benoy Ltd**
Main Contractor: **McAlpine**
Quantity Surveyor: **Gardiner & Theobald**
Structural Engineer: **Watermans**
Services Engineer: **WSP**

The most common question now asked is what Birmingham was like before the new Bullring, and where did all these people suddenly come from? Its buildings and public spaces are enjoyed by all, and in virtually no time it has come to be recognised as the retail heart of the city.

Nationally and internationally, it has won all the major regeneration and retail awards and is recognised as a model for future city developments worldwide.

The Mailbox is unprecedented, both in
terms of scale and the range of uses
it brings together. It also represents a
dynamic approach to regeneration.

THE MAILBOX
ASSOCIATED ARCHITECTS

Royal Mail Street, Mailbox Square, Birmingham

Construction Value: £40 million
Completion Date: December 2000

Description

The Mailbox is the UK's largest mixed-use building
scheme, created from the shell of the former Royal
Mail parcel and letter sorting office. Hotels, shopping,
TV studios, offices, restaurants and apartments are all
provided in the development, which links the city centre of
Birmingham to the canal network at Salvage Wharf.

History

The building was constructed in 1968 as an automated
sorting office, but had eventually become obsolete and
was replaced by an out-of-town facility. The premises
were offered for purchase, and acquired in 1998 by
Birmingham Mailbox Limited with the intention of creating
an innovative mixed-use scheme to act as a catalyst for
the regeneration of this neglected city quarter. With the
support and cooperation of city, the project was delivered
at a rapid pace and opened in December 2000.

Client's Brief

The brief was evolved during an intensive eight-week
feasibility study, which included involvement from
representatives of the city council. A wide range of
options was tabled, debated and appraised until a
preferred solution emerged to be developed in greater
detail. This fixed the broad quantum of space for a range
of different uses, together with their disposition in the
scheme. The architect's vision of cutting an open street
through the building to create the missing link in a new
pedestrian circuit was adopted as a vital component of the
regeneration.

Design Process

There are a number of key ideas at play in the scheme
concept. Making the Mailbox a route rather than a
destination was crucial, as was the development of an

appropriate hierarchy of uses. The original building was
constructed on a heroic scale, with a 12 m by 12 m
column grid and 6.2 m floor-to-floor height, and it bridges
complex changes in level and scale. This flexibility was
thoroughly exploited in the finished scheme.

The robust nature of the building allowed the 'street' to
be created without attendant structural problems, and
it was stepped in section at strategic points to create
coherent zones within the plan. The levels form distinct
environments for the retail space, for the office entrance
and for restaurants – all of which are given their own
sense of place and identity within the scheme.

The city entrance to the scheme is formed as a grand
portal with a hotel bridging the street. This leads to two
levels of retail space: one at grade with the entrance,
the other consistent with the next level where a link is
provided with Severn Street. The retail space ends at
a generous landing where the office entrance is sited:
this has a 12 m high foyer and bridge-access to upper
levels of offices above the retail space. Lifts give access
to two further independent office floors, each 6,500 m^2
in area, with generous floor-to-floor heights, allowing
mezzanines to be inserted – a pilot scheme was promoted
to demonstrate the potential of the proposals.

The residential entrance is also sited at this point.
Apartments are located at the highest levels of the
building, using the roof and wings of the space above the
street. There is a large roof courtyard, and the majority
of the apartments have generous balconies with views
across the city.

The street rises a further storey where a range of
restaurants is provided, linked to a new piazza with further
development (produced concurrently by the same team)

The Mailbox

based around a reopened canal basin, giving access to the canal network.

The exterior of the building is remodelled most extensively in Mailbox Square. Integrated with new landscaping to address the level changes, the building has a stone base raised to the level of the portal and a red rendered element above, bisected with glazing to reflect the internal street beyond. The top floor has clerestorey glazing and a projecting metal top; the whole is lit dramatically at night. The remainder of the exterior is simply reclad in zinc panels with glazing, much in the form of the previous cladding.

Where the exterior has a bold treatment at a giant scale, the interior is based on the scale and character of a typical Birmingham street. The large grid is broken into smaller elements, the detail treated in an urban and robust manner to reflect the high-quality uses. A stonework base of piers is overlaid in red terracotta, with render and large areas of glazing for the offices; the stonework grid continues through the street as a framework for the shops and restaurants alike.

The urban realm was extended to New Street Station, with the granite surface used in the street replacing former paving. In order to reinforce the new route and develop a coherent identity, public art was commissioned from Thomas Heatherwick and Mark Pimlott:

Heatherwick has installed coloured lines in the paving which resolve into street furniture, and Pimlott a lighting scheme for the ring-road undercroft.

The design pioneered a complex fire strategy that allows different users to share emergency escapes. This was integrated with service access to all parts from a central vehicle-loading bay, and dedicated parking arrangements for the apartments. The scheme also provides 1,000 parking spaces for users and visitors, with common access points to the separate scheme elements. Clear resolution of these circulation patterns beyond the public street was critical to the operation of the complex.

Project Sign-off

The Mailbox is unprecedented, both in terms of scale and the range of uses it brings together. It also represents a dynamic approach to regeneration, responding to its context and demonstrating tangible civic responsibility: regeneration of the wider area has subsequently taken place. The scheme is a commercial success and has attracted high-quality occupiers, including the BBC Birmingham Studios.

The project was reviewed in *The Architects' Journal* on 10 May 2001, and is the subject of a CABE Case Study. Amongst other honours, it has received a Civic Trust Award (2003), British Council for Offices Award (2003) and a CABE High Quality Architecture Citation (2002).

PROJECT TEAM

Client: **Birmingham Mailbox Limited**

Architect: **Associated Architects**

Main Contractor: **Carillion**

Quantity Surveyor: **Faithful and Gould**

Structural Engineer: **Curtins Consulting**

Services Engineer: **Couch Perry Wilkes**

Project Manager: **Faithful and Gould**

Traffic Engineer: **Ove Arup & Partners**

Fire Engineer: **Ove Arup & Partners**

Landscape Architect: **Gillespies**

Lighting Consultant: **DPA Lighting**

Public Art Consultant: **Modus Operandi**

The Cube terminates the linear strip development of The Mailbox to create a dramatic new 'front door' that leads through to the canal and city centre beyond.

THE CUBE

MAKE ARCHITECTS

124–125 Wharfside Street, The Mailbox, Birmingham

Construction Value: £75 million
Completion Date: Winter 2008

Description

Hovering over a glass base and crowned by the city's first rooftop restaurant, The Cube is a £75m, 42,000 m² mixed-use development housing apartments, a hotel, restaurants, retail, offices and car parking within a distinctive landmark building.

History

Located at the southwestern tip of The Mailbox complex, The Cube site is bounded by the Birmingham and Worcester Canal to the north and Commercial Street to the south. It was occupied by several old buildings, two locally listed frontages and a restaurant which were part of the existing Mailbox development. The site already possessed two planning consents for car parking, retail, offices, residential units and a hotel; and a design competition was launched to find a scheme that would accommodate these uses and complete the final phase of The Mailbox development. Make Architects won this competition in June 2005 with their distinctive scheme for The Cube. A planning application was submitted in August 2005 and permission granted in December that year. Enabling and construction work began in 2006.

Client's Brief

The Mailbox is a highly successful development featuring a lively mix of apartments; offices; hotels; BBC TV and radio studios; and upmarket retail, including Harvey Nichols and Emporio Armani. With an area of 140,000 m², the development is believed to be the UK's largest mixed-use building, and it exemplifies the urban regeneration that such ambitious building projects can initiate. The competition brief for The Mailbox's final phase sought to build upon this success by specifying an equivalent blend of uses within a building of distinct architectural merit. Animated street frontages were encouraged, in order to draw people into and through the development and to complement the facilities already offered by The Mailbox, and a strong demand was anticipated for apartments, a hotel and extensive office space. In addition, it was particularly important that the winning scheme was knitted into its surroundings and firmly integrated with the Commercial Street area. Above all, the finished scheme was to be a new landmark for the city — a building of which Birmingham could be proud.

Design Process

The Mailbox has already established itself as a vibrant mixed-use development integral to Birmingham's city-centre life. The Cube is the final phase of this scheme and it will reinforce the position of The Mailbox as a key urban amenity, whilst establishing itself as a unique destination in its own right.

The Cube terminates the linear strip development of The Mailbox to create a dramatic new 'front door' that leads through to the canal and city centre beyond. The building is firmly knitted into its context and actively draws people through the site, hopefully becoming a new pedestrian hub in the process. Extensive studies of possible routes across the site quickly defined the essential plan of the building as a square, with public space at its heart and a diagonal axis dividing it into two L-shaped structures at lower levels. As the building rises, floorplates bridge the gaps between the two L-shaped forms while maintaining a central lightwell at the heart of the structure, before terracing back at the uppermost levels to embrace a courtyard that now occupies fully a third of the plan area.

The resulting building offers approximately 44,000 m² of accommodation, housing a rich mix of shops, bars, cafés, offices, apartments and a boutique hotel and restaurant. The lower levels are dedicated to retail, with café-bars

ALL IMAGES ON THIS SPREAD GMJ

and restaurants animating the canalside. Offices, apartments and a hotel occupy the levels above, and a skyline restaurant offers panoramic views over the city. The internal courtyard will be a shared focus for the building's mixed community and an exciting destination in its own right. This space is created by an asymmetrical lightwell that twists as it rises upward, slicing through the floorplates to create a dynamic set of spatial relationships, while drawing natural light deep into the building's heart.

The façade of The Cube is as visually exciting as its form. An anodised aluminium modular system creates a fretwork screen for the exterior, while the internal courtyard spaces are lined with finely detailed glass. Where the elevation wraps around the courtyard at the upper levels of the building, the cladding dissolves into a filigree screen that provides a sense of enclosure while allowing fresh air and views through. Together, the intricate exterior tessellations and the glowing, gem-like courtyard evoke Birmingham's strong manufacturing and engineering tradition, as well as its jewellery and watchmaking heritage. The façade also plays a key role in the building's environmental strategy, offering flexibility and limiting solar gain.

Project Sign-off

The Mailbox has been a catalyst for regeneration, and The Cube will build on and further develop this important work. With its cutting-edge design, rich mix of uses and creation of a new convergence point connecting Commercial Street to the canalside and the city centre, the new building is pivotal to Birmingham's continued revitalisation. The powerful geometric form and shimmering texture of The Cube will complement The Mailbox building and introduce a distinctive new presence to the city skyline.

PROJECT TEAM

Client: **Birmingham Development Company Ltd**
Architect: **Make Architects**
Main Contractor: **Build Ability Ltd**
Hoare Lea
Atkins
Buro Happold
RWDI Anemos
Faithful + Gould
Faber Maunsell Fire
Goodwill Associates

URBAN REGENERATION

While many of the projects featured in this book have helped bring about significant changes to their local communities and immediate environs, most have not been designed with the specific intention of reinventing or changing entire neighbourhoods.

CRAIG HOLMES/IMAGES OF BIRMINGHAM

The schemes in this section are therefore distinguished by the way in which they have sought to bring new life to previously run-down and neglected areas. Several of these projects, such as Park Central and Eastside, are truly huge in scale, covering dozens of hectares of inner-city Birmingham. Others, such as Fort Dunlop and the Custard Factory, have been much more focused but have had, or are anticipated to have, truly transformative effects on large areas of the city.

The strength of all these projects lies in the way in which their ambitious strategic scope has been carried through to excellent design implementation. Park Central is focused on the reinvention of a depressed and underprivileged former 1960s council estate: the notorious Lee Bank Estate southwest of the city centre. However, unlike so many other similar projects, Park Central has benefited from consistently high and rigorous design standards. The revitalised neighbourhood is not graced with individual 'landmark' projects, but rather demonstrates a clear and coherent understanding of good urban-design principles, with human-scale streets, parks and squares. The result is a mix of private and affordable social housing that doesn't create a sense of social exclusion or separation. It can be reasonably expected that Park Central will form a genuinely vibrant interface between the exclusive suburb of Edgbaston and the neighbouring, traditionally working-class estates.

One project that has maybe contributed most to the regeneration of Birmingham's historic Irish Quarter is Glenn Howells's ingenious Custard Factory conversion project in Digbeth. This huge complex of small and affordable office and studio units is not only extremely successful, but has gone on to become a model for similar developments across Europe. The Custard Factory is a virtual city within a city, with its own shops, restaurants and very distinctive character. Home to the renowned Medicine Bar, it has provided a much-needed physical and spiritual heart for the city's creative communities. Its success has attracted others to move into the Irish Quarter. The Ikon Gallery has recently opened a temporary exhibition space on nearby Fazeley Street, close to The Bond, an earlier but significant predecessor of the Custard Factory. Meanwhile, Kinetic AIU's Warwick Bar masterplan for ISIS promises to turn the momentum of the Custard Factory into a full-scale transformation of the Irish Quarter.

These projects are complemented by significant infrastructure improvements, most notably – and critically – the proposal for a new gateway at the city's notoriously unwelcoming New Street Station. This scheme, designed by John McAslan + Partners, has the potential to transform perceptions of the city and help restore the coherency of part of the city centre that was obliterated during the misguided planning of the 1960s. A 'new New Street' would for many people be the final proof of success in Birmingham's radical and extensive period of urban regeneration.

Creating sustainable neighbourhoods
with clear and distinctive characters
was seen as essential to the success
of the regeneration.

PARK CENTRAL
GARDNER STEWART ARCHITECTS

Park Central (former Lee Bank Estate), Bath Row, Birmingham

Construction Value: Approx £200 million
Completion Date: 2012

Description

Park Central is a mixed-use regeneration project of
around 185,000 m², containing new homes, offices,
shops and leisure facilities. Its defining characteristic is a
central parkland of around 3 hectares offering a unique
and complementary quarter to the city. High-quality
townscape is reinforced by architecture of distinction, and
residents will benefit from high levels of amenity.

History

Prior to the redevelopment that took place during the
1960s, the Lee Bank Estate was a neighbourhood of run-
down terraced housing with a close network of streets
and alleyways. Within the residential street pattern there
was a mixture of local businesses and amenities such as
shops, pubs and schools.

Lee Bank was redeveloped during the 1960s and 70s,
providing a mixture of low-, medium- and high-rise
houses and apartments. However, by the late 1990s
the estate had become run down and was in need of
regeneration. It was at this time that a competition
was set up by Birmingham City Council and Optima
Community Association to find a private-sector partner
to begin implementing a new mixed-tenure, mixed-use
development.

Client's Brief

Creating sustainable neighbourhoods with clear and
distinctive characters was seen as essential to the
success of the regeneration. This required a cohesive,
flexible and robust masterplan to guide and coordinate
development well into the future.

The key objectives of the Park Central Regeneration
programme are as follows:

- create a highly individual townscape, unique to Park
  Central;

- provide architecture that is modern and distinctive,
  with unlimited longevity;

- achieve a step-change in perception and value that
  creates the ability to invest money back into the
  project for the betterment of the wider area;

- capitalise on proximity to the city centre and improve
  on connections;

- provide a balanced community, with opportunities for
  local employment and leisure;

- create a range of tenures and dwelling sizes that
  offers diversity and choice;

- develop buildings that have a long life expectancy
  – removing the need for continuous regeneration;

- create an attractive, safe and pedestrian-friendly
  environment;

- achieve a transformation of the area by the full, active
  involvement of local residents.

Design Process

The site represented a significant challenge: it sloped at
a gradient of 1 in 8, bus access was impossible, existing
residents felt isolated, the public realm was a no-go area,
there was no townscape merit whatsoever and it suffered
the stigma of a failed 1960s estate. It became apparent
at the masterplan stage that a central park would add
vitality to the public realm and value to the development.
The park subsequently became the defining characteristic
for the whole development. The masterplanning stage
of the design, therefore, needed to allow the park to

take on various functions dependent on context. It also had to provide a cohesive means of managing levels, access and usefulness of the open space, resulting in a continuous 'terraced garden' all around the parkland with a flat area for active use in the centre.

The defining characteristics at a detailed architectural level are as follows:

- architectural progression between distinct character areas tightly controlled, to offer a balance of cohesiveness and diversity;

- managing high-density with a mix of traditional and mews house-types and apartments provides a solution that is pragmatic and distinctive;

- the design is 'tenure-blind' – with a high level of tenure integration, including multi-tenured apartment blocks;

- non-residential uses are integrated into most phases of the project, from corporate office headquarters to the 'corner shop';

- the concurrent build phases employ a range of construction techniques from traditional to prefabrication whilst achieving visual harmony.

Full involvement of all stakeholders has been ensured by fortnightly design reviews with a fully transparent sharing of all information. A collaborative, consensus-driven process has ensured the project makes balanced and appropriate responses to the often competing demands placed on regeneration at this scale.

Finally, though significant in itself, Park Central represents only phase 1 of the wider and ambitious Attwood Green regeneration scheme for three housing estates to the southwest of Birmingham city centre. Attwood Green is to be a fully inclusive, mixed-use urban development, focused around a series of new central parks.

Project Sign-off

This city-centre estate regeneration project is setting new benchmarks for the volume-housing industry. The competition-winning design has created a development framework that promotes innovative and sustainable buildings with a genuine mix of uses and fully integrated tenures. It has transformed Park Central into an attractive and desirable place in which to live.

Park Central balances the need for repetition and standardisation with that of creating a mix of accommodation types, density, townscape and architectural diversity that can only be achieved by bespoke design solutions. It proves that visionary design and development pragmatics can, and should, happily coexist.

PROJECT TEAM

Client: **Crest Nicholson, Optima Community Association, Birmingham City Council**

Architect: **Gardner Stewart Architects**

Main Contractor: **Crest Nicholson Residential (Midlands) Ltd**

Quantity Surveyor: **Crest Nicholson Residential (Midlands) Ltd**

Structural Engineer: **Curtins Consulting**

Services Engineer: **Couch Perry & Wilkes**

Highway and Civil Engineer: **Faber Maunsell**

CDM Coordinator: **LAIMS Group Services Ltd**

Landscape Architect (Parks): **The Landscape Practice Group**

Landscape Architect: **Lovejoy**

169

Bennie Gray, the founder of the developer SPACE, bought the former Birds Custard Factory in the late 1980s and since then has been turning it into Birmingham's alternative retail and arts quarter.

CUSTARD FACTORY

GLENN HOWELLS ARCHITECTS / SPACE

Gibb Street, Birmingham

Construction Value: £5 million
Completion Date: Ongoing

Description

Refurbishment of the former Birds Custard Factory in Digbeth to create affordable studio spaces, retail units and public spaces.

History

Bennie Gray, the founder of the developer SPACE, bought the former Birds Custard Factory in the late 1980s and since then has been turning it into Birmingham's alternative retail and arts quarter, attracting some of the most interesting creative small companies in the region. The original buildings are a collection of early 20th-century industrial and office premises, lying within the Irish Quarter of the city. Glenn Howells Architects were appointed to the project in 1990.

Client's Brief

The brief for the initial phase of the project was to convert the buildings into cheap, attractive workspaces and to create an environment in which small creative companies could interact and support each other. Key to this has been the emphasis on public open space and interesting common areas, together with achieving a mix of uses – particularly catering and retail activity at ground-floor level – that animates the project. The principal public space in phase one was the central courtyard and lake, flanked by cafés and shops and overlooked by many of the studios. The lake is sometimes drained to create a sunken dance floor for club nights held at the Custard Factory.

The second phase of the project was to create a second public square on Gibb Street, flanked by a new studio building with further ground-floor retail provision.

Design Process

The design process is interesting, in that the client develops ideas – and, indeed, the brief – through dialogue with the architect, starting with very loose requirements to give the

171

CRAIG HOLMES/IMAGES OF BIRMINGHAM

designers the maximum flexibility to generate ideas that can take their own direction.

The design process from here is through comment and adjustment, and the client participates by making suggestions on both operational and aesthetic levels.

The interventions within the historic fabric have been minimal but striking, such as full-height atria and the crisply detailed Medicine Bar in the main courtyard. Working to an extremely tight budget, Glenn Howells Architects sourced many of the construction packages unconventionally, through small local workshops and suppliers.

Project Sign-off

Work is ongoing on the phase-three masterplan, which is to include up to six further new-build studio blocks and a possible landmark tower on Digbeth High Street. The expansion masterplan will aim to create a contemporary continuation of the surrounding urban grain, with simple and robust buildings enclosing intimate alleys and public spaces.

The project has received much attention, nationally and internationally, in that it is now regarded as a model of regeneration through a process of establishing creative clusters.

PROJECT TEAM

Client: **Space Organisation**
Architect: **Glenn Howells Architects / Space**
Main Contractor: **Pendragon**
Quantity Surveyor: **Paul Mantle Partnership**

> New uses are complementary to the existing framed nature of the building, and can be accommodated without the need for substantial remodelling.

FORT DUNLOP

SHEDKM

Fort Parkway, Birmingham

Construction Value: £43 million
Completion Date: December 2006

JONATHAN KEENAN

Description

The project comprises the reinvention of the former Dunlop tyre-storage warehouse building, together with a new-build hotel extension and related site works.

History

Following two decades of dereliction, the Fort Dunlop storage warehouse (which sits alongside the Birmingham stretch of the M6 motorway), received planning consent for mixed-use redevelopment late in 2002. This followed years of failed attempts by various developers to breathe new life into the landmark building, which was at one time threatened with outright demolition.

Client's Brief

Having been approached by the local development agency, Urban Splash requested that shedkm help develop a viable client brief, which could inject new life into the derelict structure.

The brief was to create a speculative office development with spaces ranging from 200 to 5,000 m2, capable of being retro-fitted as residential accommodation and with the potential creation of 24-hour activity on the site. This straightforward requirement has successfully been channelled into a bold architectural statement, announcing Birmingham's redevelopment to all motorists on the M6 motorway.

This landmark building, having been derelict for over 20 years, has for too long been a symbol of decay, and the interpretation of the brief with simple-yet-strong design moves is key to finally realising the structure's viable redevelopment. Shedkm's proposals for Urban Splash's redevelopment of the Fort Dunlop tyre warehouse take advantage of the building's greatest assets (its size, space and location), with an approach of discerning conservation

in the form of minimum demolition and the introduction of good-quality workspace.

A successful development can be realised by the introduction of a dramatic yet sensible circulation strategy and the clear definition of new elements within the building.

Design Process

New uses are complementary to the existing framed nature of the building, and can be accommodated without the need for substantial remodelling. With a 52 m deep plan building it is the resolution of the central area that becomes the key to maximising development potential, with the usual solution being to cut an atrium into the centre of the block. In the case of Fort Dunlop, the architects are utilising the central area of the plan (deficient in natural light) to locate the required fire-fighting cores and services amenities, creating sensible accommodation around the periphery with maximum light and views.

All services to the main speculative-office floorplates are distributed horizontally under a raised floor, incorporating heating, ventilation, and cable and data distribution. This effective servicing approach is facilitated by the creation of an external services zone to the outer edge of the flanks of accommodation. This raised external zone allows flexibility in the location of items such as air-conditioning equipment, without compromising the aesthetic quality of the external envelope.

The new glazing system (to achieve sound resistance and thermal standards for accommodation in line with today's enhanced regulations) is set back from the existing façade in order to create this services zone. The position of the new glazing is expressed as an architectural statement of the new building and its associated use, set within the framework of the existing structure. The workspace

URBAN SPLASH

created is unique in the realm of city-centre office
stock and echoes the industrial nature of the building,
with exposed soffits and columns becoming an integral
feature of the interior.

The insertion of this 'glass box' housing the building's
new use is visually strengthened by the removal of the
failed roof structure and the introduction of a new roof
continuing the line of the set-back glazing. It is also
expressed by the removal of former extensions and poor
masonry infills to the east elevation and the introduction
of a glass wall – transforming this façade to read as
a 'section' through the building, and maximising light
to the deep floorplates. At ground-floor level, the set-
back glazing creates a colonnade, allowing the building
elevation to be penetrated and introducing a covered
arcade for access to potential retail units. This forms a
sheltered environment where signage can be controlled,
and does so without the need for attaching new
structures to the preserved existing envelope.

The spine of essential circulation cores located down
the centre of the building is expressed both above roof

level and, as a continuation of its linear nature, in the
form of a new 100-bed hotel to the east end of the
building. The design brief for the building evolved in
tandem with development ambitions during the initial
stages of the project, with an enquiry by a hotel operator
(considered important for the 24-hour life of the site)
being incorporated into the programme. The deep
plan of the existing floorplates is not suited to hotel
rooms, and so the extension of the central spine allows
a further enhancement of the physical expression of
'core' facilities whilst retaining a clear design aesthetic.
This distinct facility also shares the use of the end
fire-fighting core, enabling the viable commercial
development of the new-build element.

Owing to the necessary remodelling of the site itself
– both to create an appropriate 'setting' in what is
currently a rather hostile industrial area, and to create
the necessary car-parking numbers associated with
such a large-scale development – the natural habitat
found on the derelict site is literally 'lifted up' to rooftop
level. The new penthouse level is topped by a sedum

JONATHAN KEENAN

JONATHAN KEENAN

BEN BLACKALL

Project Sign-off

Following years of dereliction, the deep-plan and regular column structure of Fort Dunlop are considered assets, which, with the correct interventions and additions, can provide a solution maximising the building's potential.

By adopting a clear and bold design approach, it is possible to realise a proposal which both maintains and enhances the integrity of this landmark building and creates an environment for the enjoyment both of its users and of the local wildlife.

This has been made possible by the drive and determination of all involved to realise a scheme which many considered impossible.

blanket, creating Britain's largest 'green' roof and a continued habitat for native birds. Above the rendered spine of service cores a rooftop promenade is created, with views onto the green roof, across the motorway and over to the city-centre skyline. At 170 m long and 9 m wide, this is a democratic architectural gesture, unknown in most speculative office developments but considered an essential move towards creating a successful environment for the building's users: somewhere to escape the office for lunch, almost the equivalent of the city-centre park in this predominantly industrial environment.

Signage for the building itself will re-establish Fort Dunlop as a landmark, with recognisable lettering at high level over the new rooftop promenade. The main body of the building envelope is therefore kept free from an array of different signage techniques, in the same way that services additions are limited and the main brick elevations are respectfully preserved.

PROJECT TEAM

Client: **Urban Splash**

Architect: **shedkm**

Main Contractor: **Urban Splash West Midlands**

Quantity Surveyor: **Simon Fenton Partnership**

Structural Engineer: **Curtins Consulting Engineers**

Services Engineer: **Bennett Williams**

Fire Consultant: **Faber Maunsell**

Transport Consultant: **Arup Transport**

Landscape Architect: **Martha Schwartz/shedkm**

Signage Consultant: **Boxer/shedkm**

Interior Design: **shedkm**

Arts and culture have a key role to play in Eastside, providing a means of expression for residents, artists and users of the city.

EASTSIDE REGENERATION

18th Floor, The McLaren Building, 35 Dale End, Birmingham

Construction Value: Approx £6b – made up of major developments by Land Securities, David McLean, Birmingham City Council / Advantage West Midlands joint venture (Ventureast), ISIS, the learning quarter, Eastside Partners
Completion Date: 2020

COUNTRYSIDE PROPERTIES (UK) LIMITED

Description

Eastside is Birmingham's biggest physical regeneration project, expanding the city centre and transforming an area of underinvestment into 170 hectares of high-quality public spaces, residential buildings and new commercial premises. The Eastside initiative is aimed at strengthening economic, commercial and social activity within the area, creating 12,000 jobs and enhancing Birmingham's vibrant arts and cultural scenes.

History

In 1999, Birmingham's civic leaders unveiled an extensive ten-year plan to transform the city centre's eastern side into a quarter for learning, technology and heritage. The development sets out to extend the city's successful network of public squares, spaces and streets, linking the core of the city with Aston University, Matthew Boulton

College, Aston Science Park, the historic Digbeth area of the city, and with surrounding communities.

Client's Brief

There is no single brief for Eastside. The design of the various sites within the Eastside area is being managed through a series of separate masterplans. These emerge through development briefs, drawn up by the city council, with a competitive bidding process to select a developer and design team to see the project through.

Arts and culture have a key role to play in Eastside, providing a means of expression for residents, artists and users of the city, as redevelopment work affects them and their activities. Innovative and creative approaches that respect the past and Eastside's unique heritage will interact with developments and help to create a new context and positive identity for this part of the city.

178

Design Process

With the exception of the new City Park, the Eastside project, spearheaded by Birmingham City Council, has been focused upon enabling development rather than implementing specific building projects. To this end, there has been considerable emphasis upon creating an environment in which businesses and public-sector bodies will feel confident enough to invest. Early Eastside successes included Millennium Point, the demolition and clearance of the elevated Masshouse Circus and the construction of a tree-lined boulevard.

The project represents a potential £6bn-worth of investment, dependent upon the combined input of the public and private sector. It is hoped that these agencies will encourage growth in learning, technology and knowledge-based facilities, while conserving the area's heritage. The Eastside concept is also aimed at breathing new life into the area through the development of a media and cultural sector, reflecting the city's many and diverse communities, buildings and natural heritage. Combined with a commitment to conserve and improve the quality of the local environment, Eastside encompasses well-designed attractive buildings, spaces, historic waterways and railway viaducts.

Eastside aims to unite public- and private-sector agencies to create a unique environment for the people of Birmingham, which can become an exemplar of sustainable development. Eastside's regeneration puts sustainability at the heart of the project and includes the proposed restoration of canals and adjacent buildings, the construction of new high-density mixed-use developments and the first major urban park in the city centre for more than 100 years.

Eastside City Park will play an important role in the regeneration and development of Eastside. It will be a major new environmental and leisure facility for the city, comprising 3.2 hectares. The work of design team Patel Taylor Architects will provide a focus and inspiration for major developments around the park area, and will create a vital link between the city centre, Eastside and surrounding communities.

Recent Eastside successes include the start on-site of the £350m Masshouse development; the £10m, five-storey Birmingham and Solihull New Technology Institute; and the £40m Matthew Boulton College.

Project Sign-off

The regeneration of Eastside is not due to be completed until 2020.

PROJECT TEAM

Client: **Birmingham City Council is working with the stakeholders listed in 'Construction value' above – as well as the Millennium Point Trust, Birmingham Technology Limited, Aston University, University of Central England, Matthew Boulton College, South Birmingham College and British Waterways**
Main Contractor: **Not applicable**
Each developer will have its own consultants

The vision incorporates a dynamic programme of mixed uses, each one contributing towards the creation of a thriving community and an important destination.

WARWICK BAR

KINETIC (ARCHITECTURE, INNOVATION, URBANISM) LIMITED

Fazeley Street, Deritend, Birmingham

Construction Value: Approximately £100 million
Completion Date: March 2013

Description

The project aims to create a dynamic mixed community on one of Birmingham's most historic industrial sites.

History

ISIS Waterside Regeneration, working in partnership with Birmingham City Council and MADE (Midlands Architecture and the Designed Environment), launched a design competition in September 2005 to select the masterplanner for Warwick Bar. The selection panel also included British Waterways, CZWG and urban designer and architect, Joe Holyoak. The winning entry by Kinetic AIU seeks to create an intimate network of carefully crafted streets and public spaces, which have a dynamic relationship with the canals and celebrate Birmingham's forgotten River Rea. Recognising the importance of the Conservation Area, Kinetic's strategy for the public spaces is to reveal the layers of the site's rich industrial history, in which buildings grow out of a complex landscape.

Client's Brief

The site carries some intriguing challenges, including the sometimes conflicting demands of conservation, ecology and the desire to achieve a high density. The footprint illustrates a series of linear and courtyard blocks, which run between Fazeley Street and the Grand Union Canal – manipulated to acknowledge the four listed buildings on the site. The arrangement of each block ensures a high level of ground-floor activity, with entrances to animate each public space.

Apart from the physical interventions, the other main aim of the scheme is the creation of a diverse mixed community, which seamlessly knits into the rest of Eastside and surrounding neighbourhoods.

The vision incorporates a dynamic programme of mixed uses, each one contributing towards the creation of a thriving community and an important destination, and attempting to exploit physical and perceptual links with surrounding initiatives. The intention is to create a community of 1,000 people, who would live and work at Warwick Bar. The brief includes mixed-tenure homes, appealing to a range of end-users, including families and the elderly as well as key workers and more conventional purchasers.

The early proposals seek to create a new creative enterprise hub to sit alongside MADE, the region's architecture centre, which is already on the site. The provision of mixed tenure business space will meet the demands of the local creative community – as will cafés, bars, shops and restaurants. The scheme will also be an opportunity to enhance local amenity provision, including healthcare and affordable childcare.

Design Process

The process established for the Warwick Bar project responds to ISIS Waterside Regeneration's Sustainability Charter. The project is seen as a key national exemplar of sustainable design.

Kinetic AIU are working closely with a team of consultants, which includes Ramboll Whitby Bird and Latz und Partner Landscape Architects. MADE have

also been retained to coordinate the involvement of a series of artists, who will firstly document and influence the master planning process (in a range of unexpected media), and secondly propose permanent installations within the built scheme. Liminal have been commissioned to prepare a series of sound installations as part of the initial masterplanning phase, which it is hoped will help to shape the nature of the public spaces within the scheme.

The intention is to create an intimate network of carefully crafted streets and squares, which have a dynamic relationship with the canals and Birmingham's forgotten River Rea.

Eastside City Park will play an important role in the regeneration and development of Eastside. It will be a major new environmental and leisure facility for the city, comprising 3.2 hectares. The work of design team Patel Taylor Architects will provide a focus and inspiration for major developments around the park area, and will create a vital link between the city centre, Eastside and surrounding communities.

Recent Eastside successes include the start on-site of the £350m Masshouse development; the £10m, five-storey Birmingham and Solihull New Technology Institute; and the £40m Matthew Boulton College.

Project Sign-off

It is recognised that creating such a dynamic community requires significant thought, time and energy.

The essence of the Warwick Bar project is to carry that energy through the whole process, which could last up to ten years. ISIS have set up a number of rigorous milestones to achieve this, largely driven by their 16-point sustainability plan, which challenges every aspect of the decision-making process throughout the project.

PROJECT TEAM

Client: **ISIS Waterside Regeneration**
Architect: **Kinetic AIU Ltd**
Quantity Surveyor: **EC Harris**
Structural Engineer: **Ramboll Whitby Bird**
Services and Environmental Engineer: **Ramboll Whitby Bird**
Project Manager: **EC Harris**
Landscape Architect: **Latz und Partner**
Planning consultant: **Colliers CRE**
Historic Buildings Advisor: **Dean Knight Partnership**
Property Advisor: **Knight Frank**

181

The project designs aim to provide increased passenger-handling capacity and operational efficiency, as well as an enhanced visual appearance.

ALL IMAGES ON THIS SPREAD BIRMINGHAM CITY COUNCIL.

BIRMINGHAM GATEWAY – TRANSFORMING BIRMINGHAM NEW STREET STATION

JOHN MCASLAN + PARTNERS
(EMPLOYED BY WSP – LEAD CONSULTANT)

New Street Station and environs, Birmingham

Construction Value: Approximately £500 million
Completion Date: Phase 1 – 2011;
overall completion – mid-2013 at the latest

Description

A multi-agency scheme to transform New Street Station and its environs. The project designs aim to provide increased passenger-handling capacity and operational efficiency as well as a major boost to the regeneration of the city centre. The intended outcome is an enhanced visual appearance that will enable the station to act as the gateway into Birmingham and the West Midlands.

History

The current New Street Station was opened in 1967, at a time when it was anticipated that passenger numbers would continue to decline. The air rights above the station were sold by British Rail and a shopping centre, car park and offices constructed above. Passenger usage has, however, increased significantly during recent years, such that overcrowding and temporary closures are becoming more regular. The visual appearance and image of the station and its surroundings have increasingly become a major constraint upon the ongoing regeneration of Birmingham city centre, and its physical configuration has increased the isolation of key development opportunities to both the south and east of the centre.

In 2002, Network Rail and the Strategic Rail Authority identified the physical solutions to enhance passenger capacity, but did not address the wider regeneration or image issues, nor – perhaps more critically – did they have the ability to fund any improvements. A wider transportation and regeneration project driven by Birmingham City Council and involving other key stakeholders, including AWM and Centro, was therefore established to address in a holistic way the problems associated with the station and its surroundings.

Client's Brief

The brief established by the stakeholders identified the following objectives:

- A station that provides for long-term passenger capacity.

- A regenerative catalyst for the city centre.

- Improved pedestrian permeability.

- A memorable station / gateway experience / identifiable landmark.

- The transformation of the Pallasades Shopping Centre (above the station).

- Minimised disruption to rail travel / maintain station operation throughout.

- Improved public-transport interchange.

- Value for money.

In addition to the identification of a physical solution to the problems of the station and its environs, a parallel business-case study was undertaken to ensure that the preferred design represented value for money and was deliverable in terms of meeting the funding criteria of the various public-sector agencies.

Design Process

Using the 2002 *Rail Capacity Masterplan* prepared by Alsop Architects, WSP and their design team, led by JMP, identified a variety of design solutions. A multi-agency working group, representing the key stakeholders, met the designers on a fortnightly basis and provided essential cross-referencing to the business case and the ability to secure funding. Presentations were made on an informal basis to the Commission for Achitecture and the Built Environment (CABE) design-review panel to ensure their active involvement. Ultimately the preferred design solution that emerged incorporated the following components:

- Sweeping away the existing clutter of ramps, waiting rooms, and lobbies from the platforms, together with existing lighting and finishes.

- Provision of significantly improved vertical-transportation cores incorporating new escalators, lifts and staircases to the platforms – ensuring compliance with Disability Discrimination Act (DDA).

- New, airport-style departure lounges above the platforms, with significantly greater passenger capacity.

- New pedestrian routes through the heart of the station, linking directly to its wider environs.

- Repositioning and enhancement of vehicle drop-off / taxi, cycle and short-stay car parking to west of station.

- Refurbishment of retained multi-storey car park above shopping centre.

- The dramatic introduction of natural light into remodelled concourse and upper level of retailing (Pallasades).

- New access arrangements to serve the upper-level car park and servicing of the shopping centre.

- Introduction of new glazed cladding to all external elevations, to create a unified appearance.

- New and enhanced pedestrian access into the station: remodelling New Street ramp; grand stairway to replace Stephenson Tower.

- Infilling of an existing 'void' over the railway between the station forecourt and the Bullring, so as to create a new open public space.

- Minimise impact on commercial value of Pallasades Shopping Centre. The owners of the shopping centre, Warner Estates, have indicated a desire to participate in the regeneration project.

- The removal of the lower levels of Pallasades car park to provide space into which to 'grow' the concourse. The existing upper-level car park for 500 parking spaces will remain. Access / egress from Hill Street.

- The 40 short-stay parking spaces currently located to the east of the station to be re-sited at the western side of the station. Access will be from Hill Street, egress to Navigation Street.

- Taxi provision to be split – drop-off from Hill Street (former Queens Drive) and pick-up from former Queens Drive access / egress from Smallbrook Queensway.

Project Sign-off

The Birmingham Gateway Scheme has been signed-off by stakeholders as meeting the fundamental project objectives. Funding applications of c.£364m were submitted to government in May 2006. The first funds of £128m were confirmed in July 2007. Detailed negotiations with Warner Estates, the shopping-centre owners, are continuing.

Construction is planned to start in 2008, with an expected duration of four to five years to ensure minimal disruption to both station and shopping centre.

An Outline Planning Consent for the Gateway project was granted on the 4th July 2007. Birmingham City Council has resolved to make a Compulsory Purchase Order to aquire the necessary interests in the site.

The clients are confident that the scheme is capable of providing for passenger capacity at New Street, and of transforming the station and its surroundings. It will help strengthen Birmingham both as regional capital and as a modern dynamic centre for investment.

On 4th January 2008 it was announced that the New Street Gateway partnership would be seeking to hold an international architectural competition to appoint a Concept Designer to develop an overarching vision for the station's external envelope, key portals and city centre setting.

PROJECT TEAM

Client: **Birmingham City Council / Network Rail**
Architect: **John McAslan + Partners**
BCC lead consultant: **David Pywell Consulting**
Main contractor: **to be appointed**
Lead consultant: **WSP**
Retail architectural consultant: **Chapman Taylor**
Quantity Surveyor: **Faithful and Gould**
Structural Engineer: **WSP**
Services Engineer: **WSP**
Project Manager: **Turner and Townsend**
CDM Contractor: **Turner and Townsend**
Business case advisor: **Steer, Davis and Gleade**
Finance consultant: **Deloitte**
Construction advisor: **Sir Robert McAlpine**
Fire safety advisor: **Norman, Disney and Young**
Transport consultant: **Scott Wilson**
Commercial advisor: **Jones Lang Lasalle**

Towers are part of the still-life composition
of a city's skyline, and Birmingham has
designated Arena Square as a place for such
towering identity.

V BUILDING

CIVICARTS / ERIC R. KUHNE & ASSOCIATES
SCOTT BROWNRIGG ARCHITECTS, EXECUTIVE ARCHITECTS.

Suffolk Street, Queensway, Birmingham

Construction Value: £150 million
Completion Date: September 2009

Description

The 50-storey landmark tower will be mainly residential
and consist of 600 apartments, including a choice of
studio, one, two and three bedrooms as well as 60 suites
with access to the spa, resident's library and private
reception rooms, including an exclusive club room. There
will feature a sky bar and observation deck on the top
floor with breathetaking views of the city, as well as a
number of bars and restaurants on the ground floor.

The V Building will be a landmark for the Arena Central
development, rising to 150 m tall and part of a 2.3 m²
of mixed-use regeneration project bringing grade-A
office accommodation, luxury residential apartments,
retail, leisure and up to 2,100 car parking spaces.

History

Towers are part of the still-life composition of a
city's skyline, and Birmingham has designated Arena
Square as a place for such towering identity. Motorway
approaches will use this tower as a navigational marker
for all who approach the UK's second city.

Client's Brief

To create the tallest residential tower in Birmingham.
To design an architectural icon that would add to
Birmingham's skyline and would be a showcase of civic
design principles. Working with the Planning Department
and the City Council, this site was designated as a
landmark location for the City of Birmingham slated for
one of the tallest structures in the City.

Design Process

Layers of silver and champagne lattice break the form
into gossamer façade planes that slip beside each other
to increase the perception of height. Drawn from the

intricacy and grace of the filigree and lacework of some of Birmingham's finer buildings, the V-Tower becomes an 'evening gown' in a muscular town. The roofline is a scissor intersection of diagonal parapets, designed to create a strong silhouette during the day. At night, the shards of light that rise on each end of the tower meet the illuminated parapets to establish a striking, elegant presence on the skyline.

Developed by Dandara, the V-Tower has a commanding civic presence as well. Built next to the Alpha tower, these two buildings share a redeveloped civic plaza that will include new pavement patterns and landscaping. Light wands in the plaza, nearly 3.5 m in height, will be etched with quotations from the literature of the Midlands that speak of the character of life in the centre of the United Kingdom. This Light-Garden will restore the storytelling quality of architecture in the heart of Birmingham.

Engaging the city on its civic plaza, the V-Tower embraces the street and public realm. As a grand civic gesture, the top and ground planes of the V-Tower are returned to the citizens of Birmingham. Offering commanding views across the midlands, a new Observatory Bar will crown the V-Tower, open to all. On the ground plane, the first two floors will be open to the public as a grand lobby reception room, restaurant, café and lounge.

The heart of the V-Tower is the collection of premier residential apartments numbering nearly 700 units. These will have striking views of the skyline of Birmingham. Two-thirds of the way up the north face of the tower, diagonal balconies turn and face towards the City Hall and Victoria Square. Balancing the generous civic spaces of the lobby and observatory, this architectural loggia will create a series of apartments that look out over the city while offering a counterpoint to the repetitive façades elsewhere.

The sculpting, lighting, detailing, design and finishing will be a recognisable silhouette. It will become part of the identity of Birmingham, distinct from the other cities in the world.

ALL IMAGES ON THIS SPREAD ERIC R KUHNE & ASSOCIATES/CIVICARTS

Project Sign-off

We have lost the pageantry of skylines. What once were symbols of faith, emblems of power, icons of pride or monuments to cultural legacy have been distorted into banal commercial identities and mechanical penthouses masquerading as art. Dandara's V-Tower will create a new identity for Birmingham anchored as much in its past as its future. All of these civic elements will be restored in the V-Tower to honour the legacy of Birmingham's architectural and civic heritage as much as capture the spirit of our own time.

PROJECT TEAM

Client: **Dandara Ltd**
Development Partner: **Arena Central Developments LLP**
Concept Architect: **Eric R. Kuhne & Associates/CivicArts**
Structural Engineer: **Ove Arup & Partners**
M & E Engineer: **Hoare Lea & Partners**
Planning Consultants: **AIMS**
Sustainability Consultants: **Hoare Lea & Partners**
Consultants: **Scott Brownrigg Architects,**
Gardiner & Theobald,
Shopping Centre Solutions

04
SHAPING THE FUTURE

'Birmingham needs a masterplan.'
Ken Shuttleworth

The Birmingham of today is unrecognisable from that of
20 years ago, and yet there are still huge opportunities to
improve the city over the coming decades. This chapter
outlines the challenges facing Birmingham and the various
strategies and projects being adopted to address them.
With a wide variety of initiatives, ranging from small scale
residential developments through to an ambitious new city
centre masterplan, there are high hopes for what can be
achieved.

Cities now compete for positive perceptions and investment in a global market, in which an ever-increasing premium is attached to the importance of architecture. Birmingham has made a huge effort to change its image and improve its urban environment over the past two decades, but there is now a strong sense that the city really needs to move up a gear in terms of quality and imagination. What has been achieved so far has been good, but how much of the new Birmingham really inspires delight and wonder? To bring about a step change, the city will need to continue to foster a culture in which architecture and design are highly valued. Birmingham has a long tradition of making good use of its own architectural practices, even for prestige cultural projects. From the 1950s through to the 1970s, John Madin's practice was the towering presence within the city, while during the 1980s and 1990s Associated Architects emerged as the city's premier practice, winning countless RIBA awards and providing Birmingham with some of its best and most thoughtful modern architecture. Since then the competition has increased, with Glenn Howells Architects having risen to national prominence via a string of projects including the Timber Wharf development in Manchester and the Stirling Prize-nominated Savill Gardens visitor building at Windsor.[1] Meanwhile Bryant Priest Newman, Sjolander da Cruz and D5 Architects have also all been building strong reputations for good design, both within the region and farther afield. A further promising development came with Ken Shuttleworth's decision to open a Birmingham office for his practice, Make, in 2005. The long-term future of architecture within Birmingham will not only depend upon the strength of these practices, but also upon the city's school of architecture. Nowhere that aspires to become a great European city can succeed without good architects and a thriving architecture school. Having been through a difficult period in recent years, the Birmingham School of Architecture has moved from its remote campus at Perry Barr to the heart of the city at Gosta Green, alongside Aston University. The new central location has raised the school's profile and should help attract more and better applicants and staff. Making sure that the city is producing and attracting architectural talent now and into the future needs to be part of the agenda that Birmingham pursues as it moves forward. As has been seen in other cities, a strong and vocal architectural community has a vital part to play in raising aspirations and standards. In cities such as Rotterdam and Barcelona, architectural exhibitions, debates and competitions are almost a way of life. Birmingham, in marked contrast, has not hosted a major architecture exhibition since New British Architecture at the Ikon Gallery in 1995.[2] If the city does genuinely aspire to becoming a truly respected European regional capital, it is vital that Birmingham's politicians and business people support architectural education and design culture in the widest possible sense. By these criteria, and even by comparison with some of its nearest UK competitors such as Manchester and Glasgow, Birmingham still has some considerable distance to travel.

The impact of Future Systems' Selfridges building has already been noted in this book. It has done a huge amount to raise the profile of Birmingham and to create a debate about what constitutes good architecture within the city. Whether people like the building or not, it has shaken up perceptions of Birmingham and changed expectations within the city. No other Birmingham building has ever received so much media attention, and none has so openly challenged the ordinary citizen's concept of what architecture can be. Selfridges is not, of course, an answer to all of Birmingham's needs. It is a one-off, eye-catching statement that has caught the imagination of people around the world, but it does not represent a model of how to build an entire city. Glenn Howells in particular has been vocal in articulating the argument against placing too great an emphasis upon this kind of 'landmark' and 'iconic' architecture. Howells is heavily committed

< Birmingham School of
Architecture at Goster
Green
UCE

ᵛ Entrance to the Custard
Factory's main courtyard
PAUL WARD/IMAGES OF
BIRMINGHAM

to helping create a robust urban fabric against which occasional standout buildings actually work more effectively.
'What Birmingham needs now is the confidence to be itself, not to look outside for precedents but to develop its own
story', says Howells. His argument revolves around the need to rebuild the damage done to Birmingham's urban fabric
rather than fixating on 'landmarks' that rarely live up to expectations. What Birmingham needs, argues Howells, is
many more high-quality background buildings to restore the rich tapestry of urban life, of which all cities are made.
Birmingham's particular approach can and should be different, but it must include a strong sense of what makes other
great Europeans cities successful – high-quality public space, a strong vision and an insistence upon good architecture.

Graham Morrison, one of the architects behind Brindleyplace, echoed Howells' concerns when he said 'I think a design that sets out with the conscious intention of being Iconic is unworthy.'[3] It is the quality of their architecture and urban design that distinguishes great cities, and Birmingham, as much as any other British city, needs to beware the hyperbole of marketing executives. When a developer proclaims that their latest project will be 'world class' or a 'landmark', the city must be able to distinguish mediocrity from genuinely good design.

Ken Shuttleworth gives the quality of Birmingham's new buildings short shrift in his contribution to this book. Perhaps he is overly critical, but the stark truth is that the city has not done as well as it should have. It is perhaps because Birmingham has become so used to lazy insults over the decades that it has grown accustomed to ignoring its critics. So, regardless of what others say the city will continue changing in the way it sees best fit. But the question remains as to whether Birmingham can now make a lasting break with the mediocrity that has characterised its urban design and architecture in the past. For a city that many had written off 20 years ago the economic transformation of the past two decades has been remarkable, but, taking the city building by building, the quality has all too often been lacking.

∧ The Pod - VIVID's
flexible editing
suite in the
proposed Media
Quarter
CHRIS WEBB

As Birmingham-based architect Bob Ghosh observes of the city, 'The next 20 [years] are going to be amongst its most important'. The challenge will be not just to maintain levels of investment but to ensure that the design aspirations for the city's new buildings match the rhetoric from its leaders. Now that Birmingham has demonstrated its ability to attract investors in shopping malls, prestige office developments and exclusive apartment blocks, it has reached a point where it needs to prove its ability to build in a way that not only fuels consumption but also sustains communities and cultures.

As elsewhere in Britain, while many people have prospered in Birmingham over the past decade there remain large sections of the population for whom house-price increases and new prestige developments have been of less direct benefit. In the 1980s and 90s, the city's main concern was to attract private investment and stimulate growth, particularly in the residential sector, sometimes at the expense of design quality. Today, there is a growing appreciation that economic gains need to be matched by a stronger commitment to good architecture and to social and cultural improvements that can be enjoyed by all of the people of Birmingham. As the effect of breaking down the Inner Ring Road spreads investment outwards into the fringes of the city centre, there are positive signs that the next wave of regeneration will be more diverse and inclusive. One of the most interesting examples of how this new agenda may evolve can be found in Digbeth, where the new Bullring shopping centre has reconnected an entire area to the city centre for the first time in decades. Digbeth was the area where the town was born in the Middle Ages, and which for centuries served as its central focus. The city council have been developing an ambitious strategy that envisages Digbeth becoming an extension of the Hilderbrandt Report's network of inner-city neighbourhoods. Because of its role as a focus for Irish immigration – part of Digbeth is now also known as the 'Irish Quarter' – and to bolster the area's historical links, investment is being sought both from Ireland and from within Birmingham's own Irish business community. There is already one Irish community housing association providing homes for the elderly, and the Birmingham Irish Forum is playing a key role in the regeneration process. It is hoped that the new quarter will eventually have 1,500 new flats, with a mix of housing-association and private accommodation. The Irish Quarter has the potential to become Birmingham's most dynamic and diverse district. The success of the Custard Factory and its precursor, the Bond, has already shown that there is no shortage of businesses keen to move into the area. It has also demonstrated that there is money to be made from catering for the kind of small independent enterprises that give a city a real sense of identity. Birmingham needs its high-street chains, but it also needs to promote more diverse and independent retailers. The Custard Factory is home to a number of specialist shops and quirky cafés of the sort that are not often found elsewhere in the city, and the Irish Quarter strategy aims to help encourage more of these small businesses. Tony Corbett, the developer behind the Abacus Building redevelopment on Bradford Street, thinks that the transformation of the Irish Quarter will take up to a decade to complete, but that the results will be worth it.

> The most pleasing thing is that all the people involved, the developers, the architects, the lawyers, the builders and the housing association, are from the city. It's like Birmingham rebuilding Birmingham and it gives tremendous pride to be involved.[4]

If the model adopted by Tony Corbett can be repeated elsewhere, then there is every prospect that Digbeth will become exactly the kind of diverse and enterprising inner-city district that Birmingham needs.

v Residential development continues
apace in the city centre
CRAIG HOLMES/IMAGES OF BIRMINGHAM

^ Patel Taylor's proposals for the new City
Park at Eastside
PATEL TAYLOR

∧ BPN's St. Anne's Court
proposals
BRYANT PRIEST NEWMAN

∧ BPN's live-work units on
Moseley Street
BRYANT PRIEST NEWMAN

Unlike some other parts of the city centre the Irish Quarter has never faced wholesale demolition and clearance, meaning that much of its essential character has been preserved. Its robust street plan and backdrop of solid industrial architecture provide an opportunity for architects to combine sympathetic refurbishment with bold new interventions. Central to the Digbeth vision is the idea of working with and developing the existing buildings and local businesses, rather than demolishing everything and starting from scratch. Leading Birmingham practice Bryant Priest Newman are working on a number of schemes in the Irish Quarter, including a plan to convert a disused box factory on Moseley Street into 57 flats and ground-floor commercial units. All BPN's projects seek to respect the existing architectural vocabulary while also making exciting contemporary insertions. Their proposals for the 1910 Harrison Drape Factory work sympathetically with the existing structure, while the practice's St Anne's Court scheme echoes the form of the adjacent church to create a series of striking residential blocks around four courtyard spaces. BPN's work points to the direction in which the area may develop, with a mixture of small business units and more affordable housing. Practice director, Richard Newman, identifies mixed-use as a defining characteristic of the new quarter: 'This part of town is very industrial but industry has started to struggle. Residential and commercial development is a way to kick-start the economy and a lot of schemes now include commercial units.'[5]

Elsewhere in Digbeth, Kinetic AIU's proposed Shoemakers' Yard development on Bradford Street and their evolving Warwick Bar masterplan offer further examples of how to rehabilitate old buildings while also bringing in good new contemporary additions. Kinetic AIU demonstrate a feel for the kind of architecture that Birmingham so often lacks — buildings that are at once uncompromisingly modern and yet still entirely sympathetic to their context. Too much of what has been built elsewhere in the city over the past decade lacks an appreciation of the uniqueness of place or context that the Irish Quarter requires. Despite the very distinctive characteristics of areas such as the Jewellery Quarter and Digbeth there have only been a few projects that showed real sensitivity to these qualities. Warwick Bar, with its strong mix of social and private housing with commercial and arts uses, is the most promising example yet of an enlightened developer, ISIS, understanding the commercial potential that exists in tapping into the area's unique charm. Since the late 1980s, innovative commercial developments such as the Bond and the Custard Factory have become a focus for the creative industries. However, Birmingham has lagged behind some other cities in fostering this growing part of the economy, and although proposals for a media quarter in Digbeth were first put forward by Ian Ritchie Architects in 1989, progress in implementing this vision was initially slow. But now, with arts organisations such as VIVID, MADE and the Ikon Gallery moving into the area — and ambitious plans for a media village at Warwick Bar — there are hopes that the area will be reborn as Birmingham's first fully fledged creative quarter.

The rebirth of Digbeth as a centre for Birmingham's new creative industries has also provided an opportunity to reassess the status of the nearby wholesale markets area. This was once home to a collection of handsome Victorian market halls, but these were comprehensively flattened by the city council in the early 1970s: one of many misguided and damaging acts perpetrated on the city in the 20th century. Now an opportunity is emerging to undo some of this damage. The existing wholesale market is a gigantic graceless shed and, like the old Bull Ring centre, it represents a huge barrier to pedestrian movement. Relocating the market and getting rid of the building would provide the opportunity to restore truncated routes such as Bromsgrove Street and rediscover lost ones such as Jamaica Row.

Glenn Howells Architects are working on a number of residential projects near the market, and are keen to see a masterplan for the area that would connect it into the council's Irish Quarter strategy. The practice has developed a speculative project that explores the possibility of reintroducing the historic street plan to this site, including restoring Bromsgrove Street to its full length and creating a dense new area of six- to seven-storey buildings. Howells is keen to create a fabric of solid 'background' buildings that share a common approach to scale, materials and massing, echoing the surrounding industrial architecture to bring a strong and confident urban identity to one of the city's most neglected areas. His practice has already begun to implement this concept with its Southside and i-land schemes for Crosby Homes.

Reconnecting the city centre with surrounding areas has helped expand people's mental map of the city, opening physical and cultural horizons that had long been obscured from view. And, as the core continues to grow and reconfigure itself so do more opportunities arise to correct past mistakes. The ongoing process of breaking down the 'concrete collar' of the Inner Ring Road took another major step forward in 2003 with the removal of the elevated roundabout at Masshouse Circus. This gigantic piece of ill-conceived 1960s road building had blighted the entire eastern fringe of the city centre for decades. With its removal came the chance for another massive expansion of the city centre and the emergence of Birmingham's largest and most ambitious regeneration strategy – Eastside. Originally launched by the then council leader, Albert Bore,[6] in February 2002, Eastside covers a 170-hectare area to the east of the city core, and is intended to become a new quarter for learning, technology and heritage. It will link Aston University and Science Park in the north with the Irish Quarter in the south. In December 2006, the council announced that the centrepiece of this new district will be a 3-hectare park designed by Patel Taylor Architects in collaboration with Allain Provost and Parklife. The park will act as a visual focus and conceptual spine to the entire Eastside masterplan, with Grimshaw's Millennium Point along the northern side, forming the hub of the new 'learning quarter'. Aston University forms the bedrock of this education community, with UCE's Technology Innovation Centre at Millennium Point and the nearby New Technologies Institute by Sheppard Robson adding to a growing nexus of teaching and research institutions.

Eastside is such a massive area that it incorporates several smaller masterplans within its overall vision. Where Eastside meets the southeast corner of the city centre, there are currently three neighbouring masterplans in place. The first of these is Edward Cullinan's Masshouse scheme, which envisages a series of high-rise apartment and office buildings

and a new magistrates' court at the foot of Masshouse Lane. To the south of Masshouse Lane lies the site of the Birmingham Alliance's proposed Martineau Galleries, masterplanned by RTKL and comprising mixed uses including retail space, offices and apartments. In contrast to the essentially monolithic Bullring, Martineau Galleries will consist of several distinct buildings and urban blocks, broken up by streets and squares. South of the new park, and linking the Bullring and Digbeth to Eastside, will be Make's City Park Gate masterplan for Quintain, comprising 600 apartments. The very existence of so many masterplans demonstrates the scale at which urban designers are now working within the city.

Ultimately, the various 'quarters' will form a ring of seven distinct but interconnecting radial districts around the city core. To the west of the city centre, two other major schemes, Targetfollow's emerging Baskerville Wharf proposals and Miller Development's Arena Central, aim to consolidate the existing 'Convention Quarter'. These two potentially huge schemes would lie north and south of Centenary Square respectively and would represent significant steps forward in expanding the city-centre regeneration further out into the surrounding neighbourhoods. Baskerville Wharf is currently a speculative project that Targetfollow have been developing as part of the council's wider 'West End' strategy, which envisages the demolition and relocation of the existing Central Library and the creation of a new business district. A sign of the more inclusive agenda within the city, Baskerville Wharf aims to reconnect a row of four high-rise residential towers, which back onto the canal, with the prestige developments around Centenary Square. Rather than demolish the tower blocks and repeat the mistakes of the 1960s when whole communities were needlessly torn apart, Targetfollow have proposed a radically different approach by retaining the high-rises and reinforcing their relationship to the surrounding area. By strengthening links to the nearby canals, Great Charles Street and the National Indoor Arena, it is hoped that the already significant east-west route across the city will become even more clearly defined. From north to south, the Baskerville Wharf concept is to create further connections between a reinvigorated canal-side and the proposed new central library on the currently vacant site between Baskerville House and the Birmingham Rep. To the south of Centenary Square, Arena Central offers the prospect of making similarly significant changes by connecting the International Convention Centre with the Mailbox and Make's Cube scheme. The ambitious development includes plans for a 150 m tower which, in an affirmation of the city's long-running love affair with all things American, is to be designed by Texan architect Eric Kuhne. 'Birmingham has too much heritage to become a city dominated by towers, but the local authority has recognised how important symbolic tall structures are to the international reputation of major cities' [7], says Kuhne in relation to his 'V building', which if built, would be amongst the tallest in Birmingham.

The sheer number and scale of projects both under way or currently proposed in and around the city centre brings its own problems. As Birmingham has learnt from past experience, massive uncoordinated development can have damaging long-term consequences. Over the past 20 years many of the changes in the city centre have been led by private developers, working independently of each other to bring about their own projects. Where possible, for example at Brindleyplace and the Bullring, the city council has attempted to coordinate development and bring about some of its own post-Highbury Initiative urban design objectives, but often new developments have occurred piecemeal and without apparent regard for any wider vision. Essentially, after the Hilderbrandt and BUDS reports of the late 1980s, there was no new single coherent urban design strategy for city-centre redevelopment, and over the past few years there has

∧ The new
University Hospital
Birmingham
emerges in Selly
Oak
CRAIG HOLMES/IMAGES
OF BIRMINGHAM

been a growing realisation that a more coordinated approach is needed. In 2004, a Conservative and Liberal Democrat partnership took control of the council and began a major overhaul of the city's development priorities. Council leader Mike Whitby[8] and cabinet member for regeneration, the late Ken Hardeman,[9] appointed a new Director of Planning and Regeneration, Clive Dutton, to oversee the implementation of this strategic shift. Following the 'City Summit' in March 2006, the decision was made to remedy the lack of an overall vision by commissioning Birmingham's first ever city-centre masterplan. Prior to awarding this contract, a study was produced by Professor Michael Parkinson, in order to identify the potential scope and ambition of a successful masterplanning process.[10] The 'Parkinson report', based upon interviews with over 100 leading individuals and organisations, suggests that the intention of the masterplan should not be to limit developers' freedom to act creatively and independently, but rather to ensure that Birmingham itself provides more useful guidance and direction to the powerful commercial forces reshaping the city – 'certainty, clarity and consistency,'[11] as Clive Dutton puts it. Following this initial 'visioning' exercise, and a competitive tender process, the announcement was made on 15 August 2007 that a consortium lead by Urban Initiatives had been appointed to produce the new Birmingham masterplan. The process, from public consultations through to delivery, is expected to take one year, and will expand the traditional definition of the city centre to cover the 2,000 acre area that currently lies within the Middle Ring Road. Mike Whitby has expressed the council's aspirations as follows:

> By developing an integrated approach within which public and private sectors work in unison, the Masterplan will create an environment within which all parts of the city centre are linked together. It will ensure that future change and development is predicted and managed, and opportunities for inward investment are maximised.[12]

The council's strategic ambitions do not end with the city centre. In parallel with the new masterplan, the council are producing three Area Investment Prospectuses, covering East, Northwest and South Birmingham. There are already growing signs of regeneration in these areas, but with different accompanying dynamics and pressures from those in the centre. Improvement is unevenly spread, and there have been setbacks. In 2005, Birmingham received the news that MG Rover was to close with the loss of 6,000 jobs at Longbridge. Today, large parts of the massive site have been cleared for redevelopment and, whilst limited production of cars has recently restarted, it is hoped that new high-tech industries will be attracted to Longbridge, making it part of a 'technology belt' extending from the University of Birmingham's new science park at Pebble Mill along the A38 to Worcester. As this investment spreads into the long-neglected outer core and suburbs, there is a growing focus on how to ensure that the benefits of regeneration are shared by the whole of Birmingham. For many people it is not the city centre but their local high street that is the main focus for work, shopping and services. It is in these sometimes overlooked places that many small and

medium-sized businesses, with strong community links, are often based. The city council is conscious of the social and economic importance of these places and envisages a network of reinvigorated 'urban villages' based around existing centres such as Selly Oak and nearby Northfield in the southwest of the city. Fifty-six strategic sites, encompassing 400 hectares, have been identified for transformational developments, with an ambitious target of increasing the city's population by 100,000 by 2026. At Selly Oak, there are plans for a major new retail and residential development along the canal that may also include a biomedical technology park in close proximity to the University of Birmingham and the new Queen Elizabeth Hospital. With the potential for 60,000 new homes across Birmingham over the next 20 years, the hope is that new life can be injected into what have sometimes been neglected areas of the city, making them not just economically sustainable but vibrant catalysts to long-term social and cultural development.

It is arguably in these outlying areas that the need for good architecture and urban design is most pressing. Often in the past, the city saw any development as a good development as long as it brought short-term financial gain. This is no longer the case and there are signs that good design is finally reaching some of those places from which it was previously absent. According to Clive Dutton, the council's aim is 'to achieve as high a level of architecture in outlying areas as in the city centre'.[13] One of the most prominent examples of this new ambition is ShedKM's refurbishment of the gigantic Fort Dunlop on behalf of Urban Splash. This project was initiated by the regional development agency, Advantage West Midlands, as a way of both saving an iconic local landmark and projecting a more positive image of the city to the millions of drivers whose first and only impression of Birmingham is gained from driving along the M6 motorway. ShedKM have brought life back to an old structure, introducing internal atriums and a dramatic new hotel block that slices through and articulates the building. On an entirely different scale is the new All Saints Church Centre by Cottrell + Vermeulen Architects in Kings Heath, which is the kind of low-key but beautifully designed community building that perfectly suits Birmingham's unpretentious suburbs. It raises the architectural bar, without being showy or ostentatious. And in Bournville, Stanton Williams have overseen a major remodelling of the former Cadburys dining block into the company's international headquarters buildings. The design introduces striking and distinctly contemporary spaces into the heart of the old buildings, while still preserving the serenity of the model garden suburb and factory.

The desire to reinvigorate the suburbs and spread the prosperity that is so evident in the city centre is also forcing Birmingham to address some of its chronic transport problems. Travel the world today and you find aspiring cities everywhere struggling with congestion, but also busy investing in public transport and opening light-rail and underground systems. These projects not only often have big economic benefits and boost a city's profile, but also bring improvements to people's quality of life. In the mid-20th century, Birmingham made the decision to prioritise roads and private car ownership over rail and other forms of public transport. The result was a city dominated by

v A day out in one of Birmingham's
many parks
CRAIG HOLMES/IMAGES OF BIRMINGHAM

v The Midland Metro
MIKE HAYWARD/IMAGES OF BIRMINGHAM

increasingly congested roundabouts and flyovers, in which travelling by public transport was often an unreliable and unappealing option. Birmingham is currently taking stock of these past decisions and is reassessing its transport needs for the coming decades. Conscious that even American cities that were once the model for Birmingham's car-centric policies are now investing heavily in public transport, the council is engaged in a full-scale transport study and intends to integrate the findings into the new city-centre masterplan. Lying literally at the heart of Birmingham's transport problems is New Street Station, one of the busiest train stations in the country. Built to accommodate half the rail traffic and number of people that it now has to cope with, there is a pressing need to increase capacity and improve what is currently a desperately poor piece of architecture. Working alongside Birmingham City Council and Network Rail on the New Street project are John McAslan + Partners. Their current proposals envisage keeping the station and shopping centre but reorienting them towards Stephenson Street and creating a gigantic new top-lit atrium in the heart of the building – bringing sunlight down to the concourse for the first time, and creating a new square facing the Bullring. There are also well-developed proposals for the next phase of the Midland Metro light-rail system to connect with New Street on its journey from the massive regeneration alongside Snow Hill Station to Five Ways roundabout. Once completed, these two key public-transport infrastructure projects will help bring Birmingham closer to a level of provision enjoyed by other large European cities.

The city that faces these challenges in the future will already have undergone massive social change. Birmingham has one of the youngest and most ethnically diverse populations of any city in Europe. In the coming decades, as birth rates remain low elsewhere, this will be one of the city's major strengths. Birmingham must make sure that this youthfulness and diversity is reflected and celebrated in its urban fabric. The key to this will be making sure that the future of the regeneration agenda is geared as much towards ordinary communities as it is towards attracting new investment into high-end residential and retail development. Birmingham's progress in the next two decades will not simply be judged on the basis of how many more buy-to-let apartment blocks it creates but on the quality of its affordable family housing, the ambition of its new school-building programme and the quality of its hospitals, such as the new Queen

∧ Sheppard
Robson's
Birmingham
Treatment Centre
on Dudley Road
JAAP OEPKES

Elizabeth Hospital in Selly Oak and the Birmingham Treatment Centre on Dudley Road. There are signs that the city is already moving in the right direction. Shillam and Smith's extensive work in the city over several years has enabled them to build up a strong understanding of how diversity impacts housing needs. Their Westminster Road housing scheme for Midland Heart Housing Association in Handsworth has been designed after close consultation with the local community. Surprisingly, perhaps, it echoes the traditional Victorian terrace form that typifies much of the city's inner neighbourhoods. The reality is that diverse communities do not actually require fundamentally different housing forms, and that the terrace house has proved both flexible and enduringly popular. Shillam and Smith have therefore adapted the terrace to include a mixture of different-sized units; as they note, 'The English Arcadian dream is still achievable and still valued by the most diverse of communities.'[14] However, what have been found to be in short supply are large family dwellings. With much of the city-centre regeneration and buy-to-let market dominated by one- and two-bed apartments for young professionals and single people, there has been little or no provision of decent-sized family houses. This lack of provision has been felt particularly strongly in the Bangladeshi and Pakistani communities, where there remains a strong tradition of living with the extended family. Shillam and Smith's Westminster Road housing incorporates small two-bedroom houses for the elderly and disabled with four-storey, sub-dividable houses for large families. The intention, while not dismissing the social deprivation of the past, is to recreate the kinds of close-knit street communities that used to typify much of British urban life.

Birmingham took stock of its position at the 1988 Highbury Initiative event, and made key decisions that would change the entire course of the city's development. The city commissioned the highly influential Hilderbrandt Report and Birmingham Urban Design Study, which then formed the basis for more than a decade of change. For nearly two decades the city was simply engaged in implementing these reports. Today, most of their recommendations have been put in place and Birmingham city centre is a radically improved place in which to live and work. The challenge now is to renew the vision for the city. Although there have been huge steps forward, Birmingham still has work to do before it can truly count itself amongst the most dynamic European regional capitals. With the commissioning of a city centre

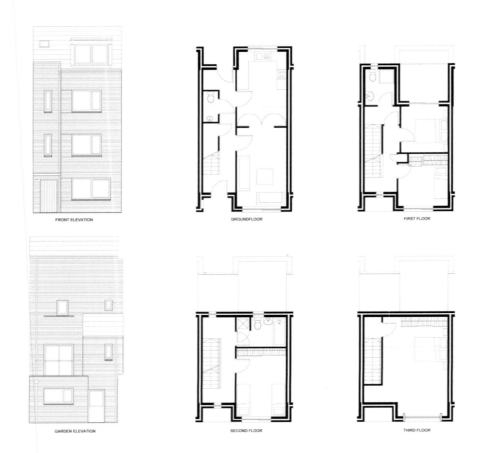

FRONT ELEVATION

GROUNDFLOOR

FIRST FLOOR

GARDEN ELEVATION

SECOND FLOOR

THIRD FLOOR

< Shillam and
∨ Smith's
 Westminster
 Road housing in
 Handsworth
 ALL SHILLAM & SMITH
 ARCHITECTS

masterplan and the emergence of the Area Investment Prospectuses, the city has arrived at a critical stage in its reinvention, when it has the opportunity to finally bury the negative perceptions of the past for good. In order to achieve this, it needs to be confident and open to criticism and embrace an ongoing debate about its direction over the coming century. Birmingham must re-establish civic pride and social need, rather than economic necessity, as the driving forces behind regeneration. Joseph Chamberlain set out to change Birmingham to the extent that 'The town should not, with God's help, know itself', and successive generations have continued this approach of grand gestures and wholesale rebuilding, with mixed results. Birmingham has now reached a point in its history where it must get to know itself better, learning to value its rich architectural heritage and building in a way that will make future generations proud of their early 21st-century forebears.

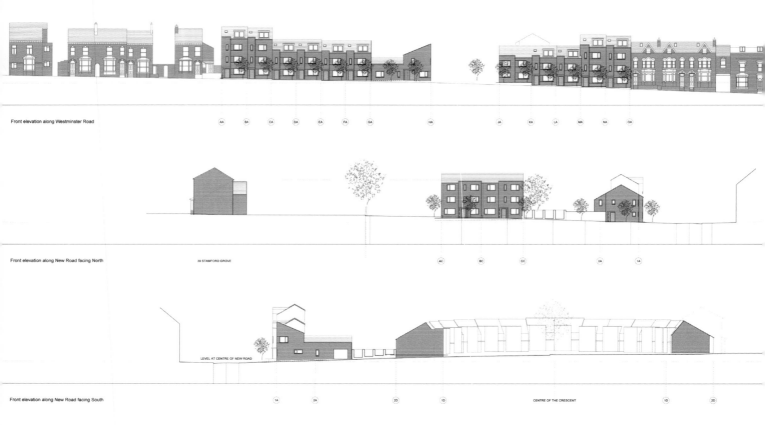

Front elevation along Westminster Road

Front elevation along New Road facing North

Front elevation along New Road facing South

NOTES

[1] Glenn Howells Architects' Savill Building was short-listed for the Stirling Prize, the UK's premier architectural award, in July 2007.

[2] New British Architecture was an Architecture Foundation exhibition that toured Europe between April 1994 and February 1995, visiting London, Plymouth, Bordeaux, Berlin and Birmingham. It was exhibited at the Ikon Gallery on John Bright Street during January and February 1995.

[3] Graham Morrison, 'The trouble with icons', speech delivered at the AJ/Bovis Awards, 29 June 2004.

[4] Quoted in 'Abacus plan adds up for everybody', *The Birmingham Post*, 22 September 2004.

[5] Quoted in *The Architects' Journal*, 4 May 2007.

[6] Sir Albert Bore, Labour leader of Birmingham City Council from 1999 to 2004.

[7] Quoted in *The Architects' Journal*, 15 March 2007.

[8] Mike Whitby, Conservative leader of Birmingham City Council since 2004.

[9] Ken Hardeman, who had served the city as a councillor for over 40 years, died on 16 July 2007.

[10] Professor Michael Parkinson CBE, 'The Birmingham city centre masterplan: the visioning study', European Institute for Urban Affairs, John Moores University, Liverpool, February 2007.

[11] From an interview with the author, 31 August 2007.

[12] Quoted in BCC press release (ref. 9991), 15 August 2007.

[13] From an interview with the author, 31 August 2007.

[14] Shillam and Smith, 'Westminster Road Housing', 2006, unpublished manuscript.

BIRMINGHAM PASSION AND BELIEF

Visions are funny things. Because no one can see them. Most 'visions' of places around the world are interchangeable if not identical. Because ultimately everyone wants the same thing. Whichever continent you live or work on you want successful, stimulating, sustainable, sexy and equitable places. Who wouldn't? So instead of visions, I am going to say a word about belief. And passion. For Birmingham.

I've got the best planning and regeneration job in the country. Not just because of the vibrant, diverse, cosmopolitan and exciting nature of the place, which is on the go 24/7. Nor because it's got everything; from city centre, inner city, peripheral estate, and suburbs requiring various degrees of revitalisation. Nor because we oversee £13 billion of development pipeline, nor that we're going to grow the city to 1.1 million by 2026. Or see the reinvigoration of our 68 local centres. It's even more than that for me. I've lived in and around Birmingham for 30 years. I've lived in five inner city properties here. My children are inner city Brummies, love the place and have had the greatest start in life imaginable here. So now I have the privilege and awesome responsibility of helping shape the future of the place and doing all the things I dreamed of as a resident urban regenerator for all those years before getting this fantastic job.

The touchstones for me are at different ends of the spectrum. History and the future. By history I mean being constantly reminding myself of the transformation undertaken by Chamberlain and his colleagues that both in terms of the city physical and the city economic was transformed under his municipal genius. By history I mean the transformational response of post war planners and engineers like Manzoni who oversaw 100,000 new homes being built between 1945 and 1970 in new communities in the inner city and its periphery. By history I mean the incredible transformational response to losing more jobs than Wales and Scotland in the 1980's by reinventing Birmingham with business, tourism and city centre living, as a formidable financial and professional services centre and the UK's second most popular retail destination.

Stimulated by deep respect for the unbelievable achievement of past city fathers we look to a future with boldness that only a City Council can bring – as it always has. Because its too important to the people that we serve and the country that depends on its success. That's why we are committing to the first Birmingham City Centre Masterplan ever, which will, in its comprehensiveness and breadth be more ambitious in scale, breadth and depth than any such plan undertaken in Europe in recent times.

Perhaps instead of a vision, is to tell a story of the future.

I want to see as many Birmingham people as possible in well paid work. I want to see a stunning new version of New Street Station, and an airport that can provide direct access to everywhere in the world. I want to build new eco-towns within the city as a response to focused population growth - interwoven with urban renewal. I want to see a new urban quarter based on the present wholesale market site based around a new city lake. I want to see a waterfall in Arena Central and trees on the roofs of city centre buildings. I want people to see the same imagination and quality of built environment and design in the most disadvantaged parts of the city as the most affluent. I want to see great public realm and stunning design in our local centres and neighbourhoods that we demand of city centre developers and designers. I want to see Spaghetti junction rejuvenated as the most amazingly spectacular post-card for the nation being the mother of all public art projects.

I want Birmingham people of all ages, in all communities to be immensely proud of their city. I want them to feel they own their city. And influence its shape and destiny. And how it looks, feels and smells. And want the business community in the city to start saying what can I do for this city rather than what can it do for them.

Overall it's about belief. Belief in Birmingham as a global force, now going into overdrive, that is comfortable in its own skin and one that looks after its own – all one million of them. And my job is to create the conditions for that to happen. The climate, circumstance, confidence for people to take risks for the city, be it in investments, buildings of ever-greater stunning design. To be creative, compelling, compassionate and challenging. To be an ambassador and enabler and when necessary a street-fighter for the city I believe in without question and until I cease to draw breath. Belief in Birmingham. Expect no less.

CLIVE DUTTON, OBE

Clive manages the largest local authority planning, urban regeneration, highways and transportation and building consultancy department in Europe.

Previous appointments include Director of Regeneration at JJ Gallagher Ltd - one of the largest private strategic developers in the country – and Head of Regeneration at Sandwell Metropolitan Borough Council.

He has extensive experience of partnership working, including membership of the team which produced the Government's Urban White Paper in 2000.

Clive was Chief Executive of Tipton City Challenge and General Manager of Black Country Development Corporation and has worked for a number of other local authorities.

He was a member of the Government appointed Oldham Independent Review following the 2001 civil disturbances and is the author of the Government commissioned Dutton Report on the creation of a Gaeltacht Quarter in Belfast following the Good Friday Agreement.

He is Chairman of the DCLG (formerly Deputy Prime Minister's) Annual Sustainable Communities Award.

Clive was awarded an OBE in 1998 for services to regeneration in the West Midlands.

⌄ COURTESY OF BIRMINGHAM CITY COUNCIL

A JOURNEY THROUGH THE CITY
MY VISION OF BIRMINGHAM

Cities are in constant flux — never reaching a state of completeness. This is one of the joys and indeed one of the frustrations of working within an urban context.

Therefore, the idea of city-wide intervention needs to be thoughtfully considered, to ensure that this delivers an inspiring framework for future growth.

Whenever I visit historic European cities, I am immediately drawn to the tight, car-free medieval streets and squares rather than the grand boulevards and vistas.

The topography and history of Birmingham would, in my view, not be suited to any grand, axial gesture, but demands a carefully crafted network of streets, squares and places, each with its own distinctive character and flavour.

Having lived in Birmingham for the last 20 years, I believe the next 20 are going to be amongst its most important.

My vision for central Birmingham would somehow recreate this fine grain and density whereby cars are kept on the periphery (and their numbers kept to a minimum), encouraging people to traverse the city on foot or by bicycle, passing independent bars, restaurants and traders at street level, with a range of spaces to live and work above. Appreciating the environmental disadvantages of a tight urban fabric, with narrow spaces, this configuration would need to coexist with a series of strategically positioned public spaces, parks, gardens and accessible roof spaces. Again, walking along a narrow street, which then opens out into an intimate public square is a real joy, no matter where you are.

Architectural diversity is another key component in delivering this vision, where streets develop organically rather than homogenously with buildings of differing scale, mass and architectural language (often sitting alongside existing, historic fabric). This can still be delivered in a structured and disciplined manner, using imaginative delivery mechanisms and rigorous controls over design which do not compromise the freedom of the individual architects.

Birmingham is an area of intense development and construction activity, where the centre is rapidly spreading in all directions. The real test is how the city can harness this intensity and high level of investment to create dramatic and memorable public spaces, as well as promoting architecture of international significance.

The planning system has a key role in delivering excellence, and should continue to oppose mediocrity at any cost. In my view the development control system could be expanded to ensure that the delivered product is every bit as good as an original design which was granted a planning consent. There are too many completed schemes that started off as a sound idea but then became eroded by the laxity of the detail design process, the lack of care and inappropriate procurement, not to mention poor construction and quality control. The quest for quality should never start or stop, but should remain an underlying principle of the design and delivery process, whether being carried out on a macro or a micro scale.

BOB GHOSH

Bob Ghosh RIBA studied at Leicester and Birmingham Schools of Architecture and was previously a Director at Glenn Howells Architects, where he worked on a number of key projects including the Courtyard Centre for the Arts in Hereford, The Dream Factory Youth Theatre in Warwick and Timber Wharf in Manchester, which was Urban Splash's first new build enterprise.

Bob formed Kinetic AIU with John Shakeshaft in 2003 and has enjoyed success in a number of high profile design competitions, including the Warwick Bar scheme for Isis Waterside Regeneration and the new Discovery Centre for Lichfield Cathedral. The practice's first completed project, The Lumiere Building in Manchester, won a series of awards. Kinetic's studio is in the Jewellery Quarter, by St. Paul's Square. Apart from his passion for buildings and cities, Bob most enjoys spending time with his severely disabled son Finn.

∨ COURTESY OF KINETIC

SHAPING THE CITY

Over the last 20 years Birmingham has transformed itself from a manufacturing centre in decline to an internationally significant focus of business. In parallel the city has become an increasingly attractive place to live and play, with more people returning to previously derelict areas.

This regeneration continues at a pace with new developments within the central business area as defined by the Inner Ring Road, but perhaps more significantly the rebuilding of the outer layer including Eastside, Attwood Green, the Gun Quarter. This regeneration is important in that it is part of the reflation of the city centre by 1,000 per cent to its Victorian footprint.

What Birmingham needs now is the confidence to be itself; not to look outside for precedents but to develop its own story. The city has within its fabric, from medieval through Victorian and modern epochs, the DNA to generate a plan that is coherent and allows it to take the next steps. Any city is an organism, not an artefact, in that it is constantly evolving and reinventing itself. What perhaps distinguishes successful cities is their ability to continue and build upon past development rather than needing to tear down and start again every 50 years.

I believe that the city needs to do three things in order to realise this potential.

Firstly we need a coherent, long-term story, or framework, that places citizens, particularly the pedestrian rather than the car, at its core. This should be a pattern of routes and spaces that link the seven emerging new radial communities with the core. This is essential to ensure that new developments reinforce each other and are integrated, rather than compete and create further divisions. Having the nerve and foresight to tackle the urban motorways that divide districts is vital.

Secondly we need to create a coherent fabric of buildings of lasting quality. It is important not only to focus on 'landmark' buildings but on the interconnecting tissue of housing, workplaces and schools which define the quality of any city. The problem is that landmarks are much easier to deliver than raising the standard of the context; however, just because the challenge is complex this should not be a reason for not rising to it.

Finally we should look at making places more different, not more the same. In the face of globalisation and the increasing homogeneity of city centres from Shanghai to Rio, Birmingham should not try and compete through emulation but rather through reinterpretation of its genius loci. The emerging districts should look to their diverse cultural mix to inform developments. At the same time the city should harness the new creative and digital revolution to drive it forward.

GLENN HOWELLS

Glenn Howells is the founding director of Glenn Howells Architects and established the practice in 1990. Over the last 17 years, the practice has built a track record as one of the foremost, innovative architectural practices in the UK. With offices in Birmingham and London, Glenn Howells Architects have won national and international design competitions and have received over 35 awards for projects ranging from cultural buildings, housing and larger scale urban mixed use developments. In 2007, The Savill Building for the Crown Estate was shortlisted for the RIBA Stirling Prize.

Glenn sits on the Commission for the Built Environment (CABE) Olympic Design Review Panel, is chair of MADE (Midlands Architecture & the Designed Environment). He is also chair of the IKON Gallery in Birmingham and advises Bradford Centre Regeneration, Birmingham City Council and Sheffield City Council.

V. WARWICK SWEENEY

BIRMINGHAM VISION

Birmingham in 1980 was a dysfunctional city: unattractive, its parts were disconnected and it struggled to accommodate itself to the challenges of post-industrial Britain. Led by consistent political vision from that time, a connected range of initiatives had a profound effect on the cultural, physical and economic form of the city. Simon Rattle was appointed to the City of Birmingham Symphony Orchestra, from which time the city has undergone an artistic renaissance. The Highbury Initiative led to the linking of city quarters, breaking down traffic barriers to encourage pedestrian movement: large parts of the city centre were pedestrianised, with public art commissioned for new squares. Community investment in Centenary Square and the International Convention Centre promoted links to the west side of the city, a model repeated elsewhere. Private-sector investment followed, providing development for new employment together with city-centre housing, retail, bars and restaurants to extend the vitality, amenity and economy of the city. All these components were essential in creating conditions for a vastly improved environment, and it has been a privilege to practise as an architect in Birmingham through this period of transformation. Our projects at Brindleyplace, the Mailbox, CBSO Centre and the Hippodrome result directly from the progressive framework which originated in that period.

So much achieved – so much still to do. Large sectors of the city remain remote, and regeneration initiatives have now to respond to a political climate in which public investment is not so readily available. There is still positive energy to be harnessed: connectivity, at the heart of previous regeneration, is increasingly important to a sustainable agenda, and our determination to reduce reliance on private transport is entirely compatible with the further development of pedestrian links and networks in the city. At the heart of transportation issues, a radically improved New Street Station is of vital importance so that Birmingham can compete on equal terms with cities nationally and internationally – and continue to attract the investment so vital to its economy. Above all, Birmingham's citizens should continue to be guided by the Athenian oath 'to transmit the city not only not less, but better and more beautiful than it was transmitted to us'.

IAN STANDING

Ian Standing, Director of Associated Architects, has been involved in many Birmingham landmark projects including the Mailbox, Brindleyplace, CBSO Centre, Hippodrome Theatre and the College of Art.

Since inception Associated Architects has been closely associated with the cultural, business and educational life of the city. Establishing its original offices in the Jewellery Quarter in 1968, the practice specialises in regeneration and renewal and has a reputation for sensitive modern design. This is reflected in numerous national and international awards, receiving the national RIBA Sustainability Award in 2005 after promoting sustainable development since the 1980s. Based in Birmingham, the Practice works nationally and abroad on projects including master-plans, education, offices and civic buildings.

∨ ROSS VINCENT

TRANSFORMATION

As a child of the 1950s, I lived in Birmingham. I have many fond memories of the place going through massive change. Vast swathes of the city were being torn down and there were still a lot of bomb-damaged sites being cleared. It was very exciting to see the bulldozers knocking old 'horrible' stuff down, and new 'wonderful' concrete buildings being built. I suppose it's what spurred me on to be an architect. Obviously a lot of terrific Victorian buildings were torn down which should have been left standing, but as a child that didn't seem important. But, however exciting it was to begin with, the city then seemed to lose its way and stutter along. Returning after being away designing buildings all over the world for 30 years it seems that little of architectural merit has been built, and, after the initial flourish of bold building, Birmingham, with the almost sole exception of Selfridges, seems to have been left behind by other cities which have dozens of fine modern buildings.

Now I feel there is a renaissance and a groundswell of activity, which will lead to some great new buildings. It is the commitment of the individuals in the new projects involved, who have a passion for Birmingham, that will make the difference, coupled with a new political will that is reminiscent of those heady days of the 50s and 60s.

We are involved with The Cube at the Mailbox, which is a unique building that will start on site later this year; potentially, the new library; a new masterplan for the NEC; and the City Park Gate project adjacent to Moor Street Station. All of these projects we aim to make of world-class status. Our clients are all committed to producing special buildings, and the city has been very enthusiastic in encouraging us to do a fantastic job.

I believe that Birmingham, through our work combined with other projects by highly skilled teams, will produce a city that will again achieve the world status it deserves. Birmingham has many unique qualities. Situated at the geographic heart of England, connected to a fully integrated infrastructure and transportation network, it is well located to attract business from the whole country. It also has a strong history of manufacturing and industrial heritage, which I believe gives it a solid engineering base for developing new skills, working alongside existing ones. Above all, it has a can-do attitude and pragmatic approach to life.

Birmingham is crying out for a masterplan which sets out a vision for the future. It needs a strategy for ensuring that it develops to a consistent pattern. All too often cities are developed in an ad hoc manner, with planners responding to the market's requirements at a particular point in time rather than having a framework to work within. Birmingham needs a practical and deliverable vision which encourages invention and creativity and allows for change. Birmingham needs a masterplan.

KEN SHUTTLEWORTH

Ken Shuttleworth is the founder of Make architects and a former partner at Foster and Partners. In the course of his career, he has worked on some of the most ground-breaking architectural landmarks in the world, including the Hongkong and Shanghai Bank and the Swiss Re tower in London.

Make was founded in 2004 as a creative and imaginative architectural studio dedicated to designing buildings, spaces and places which are as striking and innovative as they are socially, economically and environmentally responsible. The practice has already established itself as one of the UK's foremost architectural firms, and is currently engaged in projects worldwide ranging from urban masterplans and mixed use developments to civic buildings and low cost housing projects.

∨ WILL PRYCE

FURTHER READING
BIRMINGHAM: SHAPING THE CITY

GORDON E. CHERRY
Birmingham: A Study in Geography, History and Planning
John Wiley & Sons, Chichester, 1994

CARL CHINN
Birmingham: The Great Working City
Birmingham City Council, Birmingham, 1994

ANDY FOSTER
Birmingham
Yale University Press, London, 2005

TRISTRAM HUNT
Building Jerusalem
Weidenfeld & Nicolson, London, 2004

IAN LATHAM AND MARK SWENARTON (EDS.)
Brindleyplace: a model for urban regeneration
Right Angle Publishing Ltd, London, 1999

JOSEPH MCKENNA
Birmingham: The Building of a City
Tempus, Stroud, 2005

ADAM MORNEMENT
No Longer Notorious, The Revival of Castle Vale, 1993-2005
Castle Vale Housing Action Trust, Birmingham, 2005

CHRIS UPTON
A History of Birmingham
Phillimore, Chichester, 1993